CATCHING *your* BREATH

Respite for Your Soul
When Life is Hard

SHERILYN JAMESON

Catching Your Breath
Respite for Your Soul When Life is Hard
Sherilyn Jameson

To contact the author: sherilynjameson76@gmail.com

Published by

Mary Ethel

Mary Ethel Eckard
Frisco, Texas

Library of Congress Control Number: 2024913052
ISBN (Paperback): 979-8-9904576-9-0
ISBN (Hardcover): 979-8-9910210-4-3
ISBN (eBook): 979-8-9910210-0-5

ENDORSEMENTS

"Sherilyn Jameson's powerful book will change your perspective on hard things—whether you're living with uncertainty, grieving, waiting, fighting discouragement, or suffering in any form. But as we bring our lives' broken pieces to Jesus, Sherilyn shows us how God collects these fragments and begins a marvelous work of healing. *Catching Your Breath* invites readers to consider the way of the Spirit, and to learn what Sherilyn calls 'attentive harkening' to the beautiful gifts that come through difficulty. Here in the 'middle space' between two gardens, *Catching Your Breath* reminds us how to live with hope, joy, and calm assurance of God's goodness and gentle care. Sherilyn reminds us in our deepest pain how 'resurrection always follows a Gethsemane moment.' This is the book we've been waiting for to guide us out of hopelessness and despair, written by a truly anointed teacher of biblical truth."

Heather Holleman, PhD, Speaker, Professor, and Author of
Seated with Christ: Living Freely in a Culture of Comparison and
Sent: Living a Life that Invites Others to Jesus.

"In a world that wobbles between despair and toxic positivity, Sherilyn Jameson is the best kind of truth teller. Her conversational writing style pulls back the curtain so we can watch a Christ follower's relentless determination to let God have the final say about every hard thing in her life… and encourages us to do the same. If you've ever ached for someone to truly see you in your struggles, you will feel her by your side. If you've ever yearned to be more honest about the hard places in your life but didn't know how authenticity can intersect with faith, she will show you. As a trauma recovery coach, I have the joy of seeing the freedom that results from honesty about our past, curiosity about our present, and hope for our future. You will find all of this and more on these pages. Don't miss it!"

Becky Martin
Certified Trauma Recovery Coach
Adolescent Support Specialist, Life Coach
Rebecca Martin Consulting, LLC

"It happens to every one of us, or it will; we wake up one day and the whole world has changed. Out of the blue, unexpected and undesired, we find ourselves in a place where we don't want to be. We didn't see it coming, and we wish things could be different, better, or at least the way they used to be. Sherilyn has tackled this life challenge head on in *Catching Your Breath*. Grab your Bible and a journal as this must-read guide will help walk you through the fog of your difficult circumstance to see Jesus more clearly."

Bob Hirst, Retired Owner and CEO
ByRider Car Dealership

"With raw honesty and heartfelt compassion, Sherilyn Jameson delves into the inevitable disappointments and heartaches of life. Her narrative resonates deeply, offering solace and encouragement for all of us as we navigate our own struggles. Her words serve as a beacon of hope, reminding us that even in our darkest moments, grace and resilience can and will guide us through. Read *Catching Your Breath* and allow yourself to be transformed by the power of faith and the Holy Spirit in you."

Michelle Glenn
Principal, The Rock Academy

"To know Sherilyn is to be introduced first-hand to the heart of Father God. She knows Him so well that His words and love pour through every page of *Catching Your Breath*. Over the decades, she has honed her time-tested tips to pass on to us in this book so that we, too, can know Him better. You will find her wisdom, her personal practice of spending time with Jesus, and her compassionate heart coming through on each page of this book. In *Catching Your Breath*, Sherilyn chronicles how she has walked through arduous seasons and prolonged periods of disappointment, always with the joy of the Lord tucked somewhere inside. She is a worthy guide for your journey, no matter what you are facing today."

JoAnn Foley-DeFiore, Ph.D. Sociology
Teaching Professor of Biobehavioral Health
The Pennsylvania State University

"Sherilyn Jameson gives us access to various pieces of her life story and the discovery of God's "with-ness" for our journey on the road of life's greatest difficulties. Sherilyn reminds us that in all moments, including our brokenness, God is there. On each page of *Catching Your Breath,* she challenges her readers to lay down the broken and painful pieces of our lives, the need to be in control, and tells us how to walk into the very presence of Jesus to breathe again … and again. I highly recommend the insights you'll discover in *Catching Your Breath* as I have. You will see with clarity that God does some of his most important work during the in-between moments of life."

Terry B. Walling, Leader Coach
Founder/President of Leader Breakthru
Author of *Unlikely Nomads - In Search of the New Church* and
Stuck! Navigating Life and Leadership Transitions

"I'm supremely grateful for the chance to read *Catching Your Breath.* With her trademark enthusiasm, Sherilyn generously shares her experiences and perspective. She's learned to face grueling challenges with faith and hope. Sherilyn shares the keys to her outlook, along with stories and practical suggestions that will help readers get better at facing life's challenges. As I turned each page, I felt I was listening to a friend share her heart with me. Sherilyn's ideas touched my heart and helped me reach for hope in the hard places of my life."

Faith Tibbetts McDonald, M.Ed.
Associate Teaching Professor of English
The Pennsylvania State University
and author of *On the Loving End of Crazy*

Respite: a short period of rest or relief from
something difficult or unpleasant.[1]

*"In this world you will have trouble. But take
heart! I have overcome the world."*

- JESUS

This book is dedicated to my children, for their children.

Ben and Mel
Andy and Hannah

Pause often to catch your breath so that you can be revived by His.

And teach your children how to live for the glory of the
next life while navigating the troubles of this one.

ACKNOWLEDGEMENTS

"Every time I think of you, I give thanks to my God."
PHILIPPIANS 1:3 NLT

David: Thank you for always and forever believing that I could and should write this book. We have endured much together but we have enjoyed even more and have been so privileged to watch God do miracles for our family! I love you only, and I'm forever grateful for your deep commitment and love for me and our wonderful, growing family!

JoAnn Foley-Defiore and Becky Martin: Thank you for your immeasurable love and kindness. Not only have you loved me, you also have loved my words. That, along with your endless support, fervent prayers, and sure encouragement to get my words into the atmosphere for others to hear, has been a gift from heaven! Thank you for the hours spent listening to me process, reading my manuscript and offering brilliant feedback, and helping me format. To say that I'm grateful for both of you would be the understatement of a lifetime, but I am! Let's break out the cupcakes!

Chrissi Jackson: Thank you for being a kindred spirit and joining me in responding to the trouble and injustice of life with the grace and compassion of Jesus. I will forever be grateful for your faith, your love for His Word, and our many conversations about both. I'm so glad that God chose you to be the very first daughter of my heart! I love you.

Diana Crom: Thank you for hitting the pavement with me nearly every day for 20+ years! I gleaned so much wisdom from talking through my troubles, or yours, while we walked. I'm deeply grateful for those miles, and for you!

Sandy Weaver: Thank you for the hours you put into my very first attempt at writing a book, *The Heart of The Matter*. The typing and retyping, keeping me organized with a manuscript that was never published but, indeed, prepared the way for writing the pages of this book, are much appreciated. I'm grateful for your help and for our friendship that started with a neighborly knock-on Aunt Sue's door.

To the many daughters and sisters of my heart: Thank you for sharing your stories with me and listening to mine as they tumbled out during any given conversation we were sharing, or Bible study I was teaching. I have such fond memories of Calvary Heart-to-Heart Bible Studies, White Sulphur Springs Retreats, The Moving Company sessions, and the Sophizo Sisters. I will forever be grateful for each one of you and for His glory we were privileged to experience together!

Lori Maxfield: Thank you for telling me over and over (and over!) again to get my book written! You believed in and encouraged me for so many years leading up to now. Your persistence mattered! I'm humbled and grateful for your voice.

Jennifer Mango: Thank you for connecting me to Mary Ethel Eckard. Who could have known that one of my beloved former students, Jenny Ganyard, would be published first and lead the way for me getting my book into the world. I didn't see that coming but I'm really grateful it did!

CONTENTS

FOREWORD

Take a breath. Breathe deeply. It's amazing how many metaphors and catch phrases deal with breath; breathless, out of breath, don't waste your breath, till my last breath, finding room to breathe again, and, of course, catching your breath. Someone once said we can go three weeks without food, three days without water, but only three minutes without breath. But sometimes life leaves us gasping for air. Sometimes the weight of suffering feels so oppressive that the simple act of breathing becomes a struggle.

Whether it's a devastating loss, a shattered dream, a broken relationship, or a crippling illness, pain has a way of taking our breath away and depleting our hope. What makes it even more difficult is the narrative that so many of us have developed about God's absence in the darkness, His silence as we cry out for relief, healing, change, or just an acknowledging word. God must be disappointed, or I must be invisible.

As a pastor for over 35 years, I've taken a walk alongside more than one or two people who have found themselves out of breath. How they got there is varied, mounting anxiety, stress from uncertainty, depression from grief or loss, the betrayal of a friend, seasons lacking wholeness, or simply a series of difficult decisions that did not work out. Regardless of the varied paths that bring us there, the need is a bit more common. I need to find my way back to joy and peace and that abundant life that Jesus came to give me. I need some comfort, some hope, a bit of joy, a respite for my soul.

If you or someone you care about has already come to mind, this book will be a guide back to life. In some ways, more than a book it's a traveler's guide, the journal of a journey. And that's one thing I so deeply love and appreciate about Sherilyn's book. It's written by a traveler who has found joy in the midst of sorrow, peace in the midst of chaotic uncertainties, and abundant life in the midst of the hard chapters. Sometimes, someone writes words, and they are just words on a page, but sometimes those words have the redemptive power of incarnated truth. You know what I mean? Like the message has saturated their souls. You know that they have lived this truth. They are speaking from experience. It's not just theoretical, it's real life.

That's what we need as we walk through breath-stealing times. In fact, as I'm finishing this foreword, yesterday I officiated my father-in-law's funeral service. He lived a good life, but the last year of his life was an agonizingly slow struggle. I've seen firsthand how easy it is to lose our breath, our footing, even our faith, as we wrestle with difficult questions. In times like that, quick spiritual band-aids and out of context scriptures do not restore our breath. We need the words, the stories, the incarnated truth of someone who's lived the journey.

That's why I'm grateful for this book by my friend Sherilyn. My wife, Lynn, and I have known Sherilyn and her family for decades. Our kids are friends with their kids. We were on staff together at Calvary Church, so even more than a friend, she's been a ministry partner. We've had a front-row seat as witnesses to some of the hard chapters of her life. We've watched her walk through them with grit and grace. I've heard her tell many of the stories you will find in this book. I've watched her love and serve people in the midst of their own difficult stories. She's the real deal.

In fact, one of the things I deeply appreciate and respect about her is the simple fact that she cares. She cares about people, especially people in the suffering-seasons. She cares enough to go hard, all-out, in helping people catch their breath. And perhaps most importantly, she cares about God and His Word. As an added benefit and bonus to all of that, she is a great teacher and communicator!

In *Catching Your Breath*, Sherilyn extends a much-needed lifeline to those struggling to catch their breath. With the compassionate wisdom of someone who has gone through it, Sherilyn will guide you, through the stories of her life and the story of God, to a renewing peace and unshakable hope found in Christ; the Christ who is not disappointed in you or perpetually angry with you. He sees you. He loves you. He gave His last breath so that we could catch ours. With Sherilyn, you won't get trite cliches, positive thinking with no basis in reality, or dreary reassurances that ring hollow when life gets hard. Instead, you'll get more of a joy-life mentor who is steeped in the Spirit and the Word.

As I read through Sherilyn's journey, I couldn't help but think, "We live in an out-of-breath world." Don't we? So many moments; some emotional, some spiritual or relational, or even physical; so many moments where it just seems like we can't catch our breath. Let's be honest, life isn't always easy and sometimes hearts are at risk. I mean, pick any age group, from the youngest to the oldest. Pick a vocation, any vocation; doesn't matter. Every race. Single, married, divorced. With or without kids. It doesn't change reality...all around us, people are losing heart.

So, take a deep breath, let out a prayer to God for His hand on your heart. Tell him thank you for the life and joy He is bringing out of your hard times…and open the book. Sometimes life is hard, but that doesn't mean it can't be good.

Pastor Dan Nold
Calvary Church
Boalsburg, PA

INTRODUCTION

don't know when I began to believe that I could live happily ever after. I thought I could. I wanted to. I even tried to. But I haven't. I guess I could blame it on Disney or my innate optimism and the rosy-tinted glasses I tend to wear, but no matter where I point an accusing finger, I come up short. Life brings hardship. Relationships can be unfulfilling. Circumstances often leave disappointment in their wake and the chronic troubles of life are, at times, deeply discouraging. Managing disappointment without getting stuck in heartache or bitterness is a life-long endeavor. I get tired just thinking about the energy it takes to keep moving forward in the mire created by life's difficulties. I've been on that journey my whole life. Finding solace for my troubled soul has been a game-changer.

Expectations

The poignant scene is etched in my mind and memory with detail. Our boys were young when we preboarded the plane all those years ago. It seems that half my life has been lived on a flight headed to California, Arizona, or Pennsylvania, and back. We quickly settled into our seats as we taxied out. Ben and Andy were happy with their Ritz Bits, juice boxes, and a backpack full of activities. Dave had pulled the bookmark from his Joe Paterno book, and I thumbed through an outdated Good Housekeeping magazine.

That's when I noticed her in between the steady stream of eager passengers filing on board. She was sitting across the aisle in one of those awkward front row seats facing the back of the plane. Her chubby-cheeked face caught my eye, her sad expression held the attention of my heart. The little, brown-eyed child was clutching a scruffy stuffed animal with one arm and the neck of a well-dressed young woman with the other.

It quickly became clear that the kneeling woman was her mother and obviously not a paying passenger. (It used to be FAA compliant for non-passengers to accompany a passenger to their gate and parents could help their solo traveling child board and get settled. Hard to imagine now, I know.) This darling child across the aisle was gently sniffling and wiping tears from her cheeks with the sleeve on her soft green sweater. Our seats were close enough to overhear mommy comforting her by promoting the upcoming trip with words like "fun" and "exciting" and "happy." It quickly became apparent that this precious daughter was leaving to go "visit" her daddy, or maybe it was the other way around.

Regardless, the scenario is a familiar one for many, so I ask you to kindly lean in close and hear me well: Grace, grace, and more grace to you if that is or was your reality. Your story has its reasons. I get it. And far more importantly, God gets it. He sees you. He's for you. And he's got you and your family in the palm of His capable hands no matter what you've endured, what you've done, or what has been done to you. Grace, grace and more grace to you.

The scene captured my heart because it was vaguely familiar to me as well. Vague only in the sense of time; I was one of the children who visited my daddy by plane while growing up. So, it may not surprise you that when I looked into the child's teary eyes, I caught a glimpse of my own image. Not a mirrored reflection of the grown-up me, but the little-girl me who is still tucked away in the heart and memory of the grown-up me. I can't really remember a time when I didn't fly across state lines to visit my dad and his family: Easter time, summertime, Christmas time, other times. Thinking back to those airplane trips, I choked up and could feel my own heart skipping a beat as I sensed this child's heart might be breaking, if not already broken. A broken heart is no respecter of persons.

The little girl's mommy appeared to be failing at her attempt to be brave as she began her final goodbye. I couldn't help but wonder what it might be like for me to leave the aircraft with her. Would she readily admit that her head was swimming with questions and her pervading thought may have been: How did I end up here? I wondered if she would be fighting back tears or shaking her head in disbelief all over again as she unlocked her car door thinking, "This is the last place I thought I'd find myself. One place I never wanted to be."

I mused further, what might her world look and feel like beyond Sky Harbor International Airport? I'll never know, but one thing I took note of for sure; this young woman could be anyone of us no matter our age, gender, marital or family status. In fact, the same scene could have played out on the return trip for the little girl's daddy. Although the heartache housed by her daddy may have been expressed differently, it surely would be just as tender and painful, nonetheless.

The heaviness of a heart weighed down with trouble and heartache stemming from unmet expectations is all too familiar to every single one of us. Life is disappointing and, when it is, discouragement can set in us just like the sun does at the close of every day. All things on this journey called life simply don't turn out the way we expect them to. I'm sure you've noticed.

Fragmented Dreams

I've asked a question to countless women over the last four decades of teaching women's Bible Study and speaking at women's retreats. But if you're a male, don't tune me out, the inquiry is universal. It's been the exact same question to very different crowds: Who here is living life exactly as you expected? I would always follow that question by saying: Stand if your life to this point has turned out exactly the way you thought it would, I have a gift for you. The room would remain perfectly quiet every time I asked. It never failed until the one time it seemed to when that one woman at that one retreat proudly popped up with a satisfied grin. All eyes on her, I paused. But before my surprise could simmer, the silence in the room was interrupted by the high-pitched voice of the standing woman's best friend sitting just beneath her, "Jennnn! Are you serious or delusional? Your life is *a mess*!" The woman standing shrugged her shoulders, chuckled, and said loud enough for most to hear, "I guess you're right" as she glanced up front at me and said, "Yeah, not so much." And with the same grin, she promptly plopped back down in her seat. The crowd nervously laughed, and the retreat session resumed.

I have yet to give that gift away. Afterall, who of us can stand tall and say that our life turned out exactly as we thought it would, dreamed it would? Every life has a way of turning upside down at some point or sideways at another. Life disappoints with its unexpected twists and turns causing trouble of all kinds and, depending on the magnitude of the hardship or its relentless recurrence, it can knock the wind out of us on many days.

Trouble is one thing we can count on in life. No one escapes it. Jesus is the one who promised it. Not every day, but on more days than we care to admit. We move and breathe in difficult, heartbreaking, challenging situations. Trouble is a regular visitor in everyone's house, and difficulties show up much like an Amazon delivery that is regularly dropped at the front door. But the boxes that pile up don't contain orders we willingly put in our Amazon cart – not items we *wanted* – instead they're filled with challenges and trials and sorrows. The more boxes delivered, the more we fight to catch our breath as we give in to the urge to seek comfort in the overs: over-eating, over-working, over-spending, over-thinking, over-sleeping, over-fixing, over-talking, over-controlling, over-reacting, and on and on the list goes. And when we can resist the overs, we often slump down on the couch with a sigh, thoroughly disappointed and discouraged, even before the next box is opened.

Jesus Waits for Us

Trouble and hardship have been piling up on my doorstep much of my life. My journals are full of handwritten text, Bible passages, and quotes by favorite authors, inscribed by hand, in an effort to process scenes just like the seemingly weary woman on the airplane, or the weary one in me. I know I took great liberty reading into that scene, but I assure you, it wasn't much of a stretch. I've often wondered why the incident stuck with me like gorilla glue.

It could be because I journaled about it as part of my search to know and understand not only my personal heartache but also the response of Jesus to the disappointment in all of us. I've felt nearly desperate at times to know what Jesus thinks about the sadness and confusion I harbor in my heart in any given situation, and what He wants to do about my hardship.

Maybe you have too. He doesn't leave us alone in our heartache nor the troubling circumstances that cause it. I really do believe that the words of Jesus recorded by the apostle John in chapter 10 of his gospel book are true. Jesus said He came to earth so that you and I might be able to enjoy life (John 10:10). I'm convinced that the heartache I grew up with wasn't the daily bounty Jesus had planned for me day in and day out. There was another power that worked against me (Ephesians 6:12). There had to be more, and I had to know what that was.

I habitually read, reflect, and examine the life of Jesus recorded in the four gospel books of the New Testament. At least I try to. That habit reveals His heart to me in His response to those He touches, heals, delivers, and influences. Such as the time He went to Jacob's well in Samaria and had a conversation with a woman whose heart hid her disappointment and ensuing hardship. You may be familiar with the well-worn account told by John in chapter 4 of his gospel. Then again, you may not be. Either way, let's go there together in our imagination to peek in at the site where Jesus waits for a woman not all that different from you and me. She could not have known what a glorious encounter she was about to have with Jesus at the well in a town that was a very unlikely place for a Jew to visit. And although you may not have reason to believe me yet, that is not all that different than you and me. Hang with me.

Jesus is found waiting for a woman surely riddled with disappointment in the heat of the day. Somewhere along the way, life had gone wrong and, surely, she was bewildered on some level by all the unmet expectations. Scripture tells us that Jesus had passed through Samaria, but it doesn't mention how inconvenient that would have been. He was going from Galilea to Judea, which is a straight shot north. Samaria is out of his way.[2] It just wasn't geographically necessary for Jesus to go through Samaria, and anything not geographically necessary for one who walks everywhere seems significant.

Scripture says that Jesus "had to" go there, implying a direct order. Jesus came to earth to do the Father's will (John 6:38), so I think we can safely conclude this was a divine appointment for the Samaritan woman. She was there in the "heat of the day," likely hoping to avoid hanging out with the upstanding married women who drew water early in the morning or toward evening. She may even have been reluctant to socialize with those who were chatting about their wonderful marriage or family life, or about her failures or her many marriages, and more. Either way, she went to the well by herself; she and Jesus were alone there together.

There was no such thing as the "Samaritan Dream." At best she would hope to marry a wealthy man. It's easy to imagine her longing to be loved and known by someone, even after failure in relationship-upon-relationship. We don't understand how a husband could demand a divorce over burnt supper. But what we do know is that she had endured five marriages, five divorces, and was living with man number six. And maybe there had been more. It's hard to say. She may have been the epitome of looking for love in all the wrong places.

Samaritans were half-Jew and half-Gentile so it's likely she was insecure about who she was and to whom she belonged. Women had little to no value beyond the home front in her male-dominated culture. They were expected to follow strict laws concerning sexual purity and monogamous relationships. No wonder we find her at the well empty-handed relationally, disillusioned with life, trying to survive the hardship dealt her. Maybe created by her own choices but, maybe not. Nonetheless, her heart was surely packed with disappointment.

Jesus never
meets our
disappointment
in life
with His
disappointment
in us.

Noon was an unlikely time to draw water from the well with the most piercing heat of the day in a desert land. Hardship can cause any one of us to inconvenience and isolate ourselves. The Samaritan woman seemed to be embracing both, and Jesus is waiting there for her with all of her hidden heartache.

The Conversation that Transforms

So, Jesus starts a conversation with the Samaritan woman and then intentionally provokes her to admit the truth of her reality to Him ... and to herself. Avoiding or denying the truth is not spiritual, it's just unhealthy. Every single time we choose to hide, isolate, we eclipse walking in freedom of Christ and personal integrity. Jesus offers His words so that hers can be silenced, and that string of questions that shame plagues us with:

+ Why is this happening to me?
+ How did my life turn out this way?
+ What did I do wrong?
+ Is God mad at me?
+ How much longer will this go on?
+ What happens when I can't endure this anymore?
+ Why won't God answer my prayers?

The enemy of our soul has been harassing us for centuries with similar questions. Discouragement is about him seeking to dislodge courage from our soul. It started with Eve in the Garden of Eden, and it worked like a charm as it trickled down to Adam. The evil one keeps tempting us to reason our circumstances to death, to overthink and attempt to figure things out in an effort to fix whatever (or whomever) went wrong. He knows that if we ask enough questions long enough, we

> **Jesus never meets our disappointment in life with His disappointment in us.**

will eventually blame someone for our disappointment, and potentially be consumed with self-pity.

But when we, like the Samaritan woman, welcome and listen to the kind and gentle words of Jesus, we find the strength and wisdom to let go of what we don't understand and to be understood by the only One who does. Jesus doesn't meet the Samaritan woman's disappointment in life with disappointment in her. Jesus meets her disappointment with grace and truth. Is it any wonder? That's who He is. Jesus never meets our disappointment in life with His disappointment in us.

Jesus waits for the chance to speak to this woman's heartache about the truth of her current dilemma, and her good future. You and I are not that unlike the Samaritan woman. Oh, our circumstances are likely very different, our gender may be different, and we may even have a healthy and fulfilling marriage, but who of us can't relate to our soul being weighed down by countless unmet expectations?

At some point, and often over and over, we find ourselves isolated and alone in heartache, confusion, and brokenness. I came to tell you that Jesus is not disappointed in you. He waits for you to welcome His words and then watches while they transform your heart, even if the circumstance of your hardship remains the same. Jesus has respite on His mind for you, and for me.

Respite is a short period of rest or relief from something difficult or unpleasant.[3] Respite is implied in the invitation of Jesus to the weary ones. He invites you and me to come to Him when we are tired, weighed down by our troubles, trying to catch our breath. Although we walk around in a body, we have a soul and are a spirit. It's our soul that endures and navigates suffering; the place where our mind, will, and emotions reside. Our souls can grow heavy and desperate for respite in times of trouble. In those moments turned seasons, God is not distant nor is He mad, holding unrealistic expectations over His followers. Instead, He comes close to the one whose heart is breaking, or is just really, really tired (Psalm 34:18; Isaiah 40:29).

God's Not Mad

I lived over 40 years of my life convinced Jesus was mad and disappointed with me. At about age 42, I heard him kindly and gently speak to me like he did the woman at the well. There were no trumpets playing nor angelic beings that showed up. His voice sounded like mine because He's in my thoughts, and I've come to know His voice from reading it in His Word (1 Corinthians 2:16b). More about that later.

What matters is that Jesus was waiting for me that day in my minivan. His words began to change everything for me, everything in me. It was the beginning of basic training for the ears of my heart to hear His voice. It was the miracle I longed for in my own disappointment and hardship without even knowing that's what I wanted or needed.

Hearing God's Voice for the First Time

It was a colorful and ordinary fall day in Central Pennsylvania. I was driving to a local farm stand to pick up pumpkins when the voice of Jesus broke through to my heart in a new way. He's skilled at asking questions, and our conversation started that way: *"Sherilyn, do you know what I love about you?"* His question was met with my silence. I was stunned. Was that really Jesus and *did I know what He loved about me?* I nearly had to pull off the road to process it.

Jesus loved something *about me?* Oh, I knew he loved me. I really did. You know, in a very general way; Jesus loves me, this I know, for the Bible tells me so. But to think he loved something *specific about me* was unfathomable. At least until that day in my minivan on Whitehall Road.

I need to back up just a bit to give some context.

My brother was dying. He lived in Northern California, and I lived in Central Pennsylvania. He was far away, and I was worried. He had been HIV positive for ten years and his body was clearly coming to the end of outrunning his diagnosis with naturopathic measures.

I had been praying and believing and waiting for a meaningful spiritual conversation with Ron. When you are given the gift of knowing someone will soon step into eternity but aren't sure their destination is heaven, you worry. You also pray and believe and wait for a meaningful conversation about that very thing. I had done all of that. Ron left me a voicemail that morning (think before cell phones) and our answering machine recorded something to the effect of, "Call me back, Baby Sister, I have something really important to tell you!"

Ron and I talked nearly every day, and nearly every day he endearingly called me "Baby Sister." As I drove toward Harner Farms, I thought maybe he said he had something "exciting" to tell me. I wasn't quite sure but, as I thought about that call, eager anticipation was growing in my heart! I was convinced Ron had called to tell me about an encounter he had with Jesus! After all, I had been fervently praying for that very thing, and I could hardly wait to return home to call him! I was just sure this was a turning point! And in the middle of it all, Jesus interrupted my ordinary day, just like he did the Samaritan woman, to talk to me about what was on my heart and His.

Jesus told me He was proud of my faith that day. I had to ask Him to say it again: *Jesus was proud of my faith!* My faith to pray for my dying brother. My faith to believe in what I did not yet see. My faith to think this was the phone call I had been waiting for, longing for. *Jesus was proud of my faith!* That. Was. Amazing. I had never ever heard God tell me that He loved something about me before! Never. But not because He didn't want to, only because I didn't know how to welcome and listen to His words.

I had believed the lie that this God who saved me was mad most of the time, and I had believed it for so long that it was now part of my default thinking, "God's mad and probably at me." But here's the thing. When we receive revelation that God is actually not mad at us and that His Son came to earth to be with us, even in our hardship, maybe especially there, everything can change. Just like it did for the woman hiding, even from herself. Going to the well in the heat of the day. Jesus was there waiting for her. He knew she was disappointed in life, and he wanted her to know that he wasn't disappointed in her.

Jesus is no respecter of persons. He never is. And He was waiting for me there in my minivan. My circumstances and that of the Samaritan woman were vastly different. Yours likely are too. But Paul tells us that there is a commonality in the adversity we all must navigate on earth (1 Corinthians 10:13). I think that's because there are so many similarities surrounding a broken heart and attached to hardship.

Would you believe me if I told you that Jesus is waiting somewhere in one of your ordinary days, longing to talk to you about your disappointments, about the trouble you're enduring? It's true! He has a divine appointment in His books reserved for you. And not just one, but many! In fact, He has a lifetime of them.

I pray you'll encounter Jesus on the pages of this book and begin to believe that God breathed the breath of life in you on the day you were born, and the enemy regularly attempts to knock the wind of that life out of you (Genesis 2:7; 1 Peter 5:8).

May you hear Him asking you to press pause for a bit, be still and rest your troubled soul so that you can be refreshed as His breath settles on you again, and you can catch yours.

When you experience that pause and hear His words, the peace that goes beyond what can fully be understood will lead you back into your world. And you may still have trouble there, but it can be met with a confident resolve to journey on with courage and contentment in the face of questions swirling around your unmet expectations.

The sequel to the story about my brother is that he had not had an encounter with Jesus that he wanted to tell me about, not yet anyway. In fact, I can't even remember what he told me with such excitement when I called back.

Nothing had changed in my circumstances that day, but everything had changed in me that day. Jesus spoke to my heart right there in my

minivan, and I welcomed His words. Jesus is waiting for you at the well –
or in your SUV – He's gone out of His way to be there because He longs
to be gracious to you.

This book will help train your ear to listen more closely so that you
can catch your breath even when disappointment is chomping at the heels
of your soul, and you're knee deep in hardship. It makes no difference if
you easily and often hear His voice or if you never have. The pages you
hold in your hands are meant to guide you. You can learn to welcome His
words more often and more clearly, or for the very first time.

I feel hopeful for you because I know that being convinced you can
hear God's voice can change everything and give hope of a supernatural
kind. I invite you to settle in and keep reading, because you are about to
catch your breath, and be revived by His.

May this book be like a well-worn bench inviting you to sit and rest
long enough to breathe in God's breath of life before tomorrow's sunrise.

"Therefore, the LORD will wait, that He may be gracious to you; And
therefore He will be exalted, that He may have mercy on you."
Isaiah 30:18a

one
SHATTERED

"When my mother and father forsake me,
then the Lord will take care of me."

PSALM 27:10

t was a typical Sunday night when our family of six piled into our Rambler station wagon and headed home from church. Our pastor-daddy swung by to pick up donuts before pulling into our short narrow driveway. He told my mother he was going back to the church for a counseling appointment and instructed the rest of us to take our Bibles and Sunday School papers into the house. He didn't want them rolling around in the back of the car all week. Fair enough. He drove off and we scrambled into the house to eat donuts and get ready for bed, our Sunday night ritual. I only have a vague recollection of the rest of the story that night, but it has been tossed around in conversation over decades of family life. I know it's accurate.

We were obedient children, always expected to behave and cooperate. The rules were predictable, so it wasn't long before we had pajamas on after brushing the donut sugar from our teeth and headed off to bed while daddy lingered at the church, counseling some distraught soul, or so we thought.

It was 1962 and life for our family was stereotypical, dependent on routine, and very secure. Until it wasn't. Like most 4-year-olds in the 60s, my world amounted to one-day-after-another at home with my happy, beautiful, and extremely organized stay-at-home mom. The weekdays held some semblance of variety, but Sundays were reserved for church attendance. All morning and all evening with roast, potatoes, and naptime in between. Life was predictable, uncomplicated, secure. Until it wasn't.

My dad led our family and our church in North Highlands, California, a suburb of Sacramento, where he pastored a vibrant growing Southern Baptist Church. Brother Green, as most knew him, was gregarious, optimistic, charismatic, funny, a gifted communicator and anointed preacher. But to me he was daddy, fun-loving, and a very busy parent. He always had a joke to tell and something positive to offer everyone he met. He had the spiritual gift of leadership and evangelism. Daddy would talk to anyone and everyone about Jesus. No exaggeration! Even now, more than a decade after he left earth and entered heaven, I joke that he's up there still trying to get somebody saved.

Our Baptist church was growing with new converts as people in North Highlands came to church and came to Christ week-after-week. My mother was lovely and hospitable and kind-hearted. She enjoyed being a mother, a homemaker and a pastor's wife. Until she wasn't.

It was around midnight on that fateful Sunday when my mom woke up and realized Daddy was still not home. She struggled to throw on her bathrobe while scurrying to the kitchen land line to dial his office. As my worried mother waited, my daddy's office phone rang off the hook. Mom was concerned and my brother was roused by the slight midnight commotion. As Mom and Ron stood in the dim lit kitchen surrounded by the pitch-black night spread across the window, Mom informed my older brother that she was going to walk to the church to check on my dad, convinced someone had harmed him. Few families had two cars in the early sixties and Brother Green's family was no different. Daddy had the car. Our only car. A brief and mild disagreement broke out as Ron insisted on making the midnight trek with our mother. He won, and the two of them headed out into the balmy June darkness while my sisters and I slept through it all.

I knew North Highlands Baptist Church was our second home, but what I didn't know was that it wasn't just a block from our house, but more like six. Mom and Ron hustled to the church building and entered the back of the sanctuary, as it was the only access to Daddy's office housed up front just left of the baptistry. Daddy's office door was ajar with a sliver of light spilling across the front of the sanctuary providing just enough glow for their feet to make the tense, silent stroll to Daddy's pastoral office. Mother rarely talked about that night once she lived through it while my brother described it as nothing short of terrorizing. In fact, until the day he took his last breath, he couldn't walk down a long, dark hallway without being triggered. It was during one of our many heart-to-heart conversations about our family that he confided in me that with every step his tennis shoes took as a 13-year-old boy that night; a phrase hissed a threat over and over in his ears: Dad is dead. Dad is dead. Dad is dead.

He and my mother would soon discover that although my daddy was indeed still alive, family life as we had known it was just about to breathe its last breath. Mom and Ron entered a quiet, empty office with a larger-than-life business envelope propped up on the front of Daddy's desk facing the door. "Marjorie" was written on the front in Daddy's handwriting. Mom unhinged the back flap, lifted the letter from the envelope, and undid the tri-fold piece of paper. It was the only trace that Daddy had indeed been in his office that night. In slow motion, Mom slid onto the chair behind her, staring only at the handwritten letter in her hands that fell limp into her lap. Surely in shock, she couldn't have known that all bets were off on anything being typical or predictable for a long time to come. Let alone, secure. Just as methodically as she slumped into the chair, she stood up and, with a robot-like tone, said to my brother: Let's go.

"Where?" (Silence) "Mom, where are we going?"

"Home."

"But Mom, where's Dad?"

"He's gone."

"Gone? What do you mean, *gone*? Where did he go?"

Ron kept reframing the question while my mother set her face like a flint and headed out of our second home called North Highlands Baptist Church and back out onto the quiet middle-of-the-night street toward our house. She finally responded in a slight whisper: "Ronnie, your dad left with another woman he says he loves; he's leaving me." The other woman was my mother's close friend. Ron had a million questions but, even at 13, he was a kind-hearted, sensitive kid and somehow, he knew it was best to walk back to the house next to our mother in silence.

Until that momentous night, my family had been enjoying life in a small 3-bedroom house with a dad who worked, a mom who stayed home, one car out front, and enough money and food to get by. Life, as my four-year-old self knew it, had been good. Really good. The routine and predictability made me feel safe and secure and, as far as I could tell, everybody was happy and loved each other. That is until Trouble came to stay like a close, unwelcomed relative. Trouble moved in with us that night and never really left.

So, how does a family, let alone a little girl, pick up the shattered pieces and put something back together that resembles the predictable, uncomplicated, secure life that blows up overnight? Literally. None of us knew. But I now know that it's in those very moments, when the broken pieces of one's soul, maybe even their life, lie fragmented all over the place, that heaven begins the supernatural work of "taking us up." The Hebrew word for "takes us up" in Psalm 27:10 is *asap*, meaning: to gather and collect.[4] Although completely unaware, the Holy Spirit began the life-long process of gluing my soul back together, piece-by-piece-by-shattered piece, in the wee hours of the morning way back in 1962.

I have a hunch He's been behind the scenes doing the same kind of work for you too. We just aren't always aware of what He's up to.

In the World, You Will Have Trouble

Trouble can come like an earthquake as it did for my family that night. It can shake everything we've ever known off its foundation and leave us terrified and wondering what on earth just happened.

And yet, the reality is that God is the God of the mountains. He is a rock when our feet are on shaky ground and yet, trouble that visits in the form of trauma, and goes unexplained and unprocessed, has lasting effects.

I was not able to escape that reality. The wind got knocked out of me on that tumultuous night making it hard to catch my breath for many years to come. When trouble is traumatic, it needs to be talked about and processed in order to be healed. My parents didn't know that, and in their ignorance, I was often left gasping for air.

Trouble comes knocking on everyone's door time and time again. And just when you think it has left the property, you discover it's not even off the front porch. It knocks again … and again … and again. It doesn't matter if the trouble is modest in nature; a late arrival, the lost keys, an argument, the clogged drain, or some situation far more serious in nature, like with an unexpected crisis; the threatening medical report, the rage of addiction, the divorce papers, another miscarriage, job loss, an untimely death. Whether the trouble is modest, catastrophic, or somewhere in between, it is always the unwelcomed house guest that can evoke panic with just a word, a glance, a thought, a disappointing moment.

The thing about trouble is that it never asks permission to enter. It startles and intrudes and can arrest one's peace, leaving its victims gasping for air, trying to catch their breath without warning. The other thing about trouble is that Jesus made sure we knew it would be our earthly companion.

> *"These things I have spoken to you, that in Me you may have peace. In the world you will have tribulation; but be of good cheer, I have overcome the world."*
> *- Jesus, to His disciples right before He was murdered (John 16:33).*

My whole life has been marked by trouble. Maybe yours has too. I'm mostly okay with that at this point knowing that the parting words of Jesus awaken me to the reality that, while I'm still here, I'm going

> **It's Jesus in us that is the power to overcome the stranglehold that suffering has on us.**

to live with troubles in life, as will those I love. I hear that. I've seen it and, for the most part, I've accepted it. You probably have too. However, we don't like it. We so wish it were different. We're not okay with the second part of that forewarning that Jesus spoke to His disciples to be of good cheer even though He has overcome the world.

I've pondered that declaration and asked Jesus over and over why He asks us to *be of good cheer* when we're enduring tribulation, adversity, and trouble. And I'm always slightly perplexed about why James tells us to consider encountering all kinds of trials as something joyous (James 1:2). Those words feel more like that of a bully than a friend; a cruel joke of sorts as we walk through days and weeks and months of suffering.

The question isn't "why trouble?" but "why the expectation to respond to our earthly suffering with joy and cheer?" Did Jesus really mean *be of good cheer* and *full of joy* when life hurts? *That* is exactly what we have a hard time getting our heart and head around, isn't it?

The word "cheer" in the Greek is the word "tharseo,"[5] and it means to have courage and be full of cheer. My online dictionary explains further that courage as a noun means "the ability to do something that frightens someone" or "strength in the face of pain or grief."[6] Now *that* is actually very helpful! In our trouble we want that kind of ability. We need that kind of strength. It's Jesus in us that is the power to overcome the stranglehold that suffering has on us. A power that attempts to choke and push us around, shoving us closer and closer toward discouragement and hopelessness in this earthly place we call home.

Even as a temporary resident, we need help and strength because a discouraging *moment* can turn into a discouraging day that converts into a discouraging week … month … and eventually becomes a season of hopelessness. And when that kind of despondency hangs around long enough, we'll hear it begging us to give up and quit. We've all felt the temptation, it's the nature of trouble. But when we let such temptation be a warning light on the dashboard, we can be sure it's time to slow down and require our heart and mind to hit pause so that we can catch our breath before pressing on.

So, we must often give our racing minds permission to find a nearby bench where we can sit down and inhale a big gulp of fresh air until our lungs fill with hope again, and our shattered soul can settle a bit. This passage of downtime allows us to gather the courage to do what frightens us most and strong enough to face the pain or grief that shattered our soul and is chasing us down.

It's in the pause where we're able to reclaim our ability to breathe again and stand with stamina and a wiser perspective. Making room for pause is a game-changer in this race we call life. A race with obstacles and roadblocks and way too much trouble that can leave us shattered and hurting.

I've often wondered if James, the author of the short book at the end of the New Testament, really believed what he wrote in chapter one: that followers of Jesus can be *full of joy* when we are smack dab in the middle of a season of trouble and trials?

Let's first note that James is crystal clear about adversity and its insistence to test our faith. We can agree with that, we've lived it even though none of us would ever sign up for it. Adversity pushes us to persevere and be resilient in that very place that feels most frightening, overwhelming, exhausting. Persistence and resilience enlarge our capacity to get through instead of giving up. In fact, we grow up in seasons of trouble, mature as we practice patience and wait on heaven to act on our behalf. We may not like it, but we also never want to resist the way of the Spirit. So, we stay soft-hearted in response to what God wants to do in us through difficulties that ultimately shape our hearts to be more like Jesus (2 Corinthians 3:18).

We lean into the lesson, the revelation, even the discipline of the Holy One, so that we might grow up in knowing Him, not just *about* Him but *know* Him, His heart and His ways. And not in a religious way, not to earn brownie points with God so He might love, bless, or respond to us more favorably. But in a relational way with the Father, Son and Holy Spirit so that we might move in tandem with their will, so the capacity of our heart becomes more like theirs with each and every trial.

It's in the waiting, the maturity, the relationship with the Trinity where we surprisingly discover what James first mentioned; a calm delight in the trials of our lives, not *for* them but *in them*. It's in the with-ness of God where we can settle down and appreciate that He is a God who doesn't just show up in our brokenness. He's already there, waiting with a plan to glue us back together after being shattered by the troubles of life. He gathers and collects the pieces He knows are needed to make something of resemblance to the blueprint of heaven for my life and yours.

When Help is Mandatory

The night my daddy left to start a new family, although life-changing and confusing, was not what tore my heart to shreds. It was the days turned weeks, months, and years of navigating the brokenness that followed. Too often coming up short, feeling empty and longing for repair, that's what held my soul captive with its sense of feeling shattered and often helpless.

So, by the time I was in my mid-30s, married with two children, I began to hit the same emotional wall over and over and over again while relational strife began to play out in our marriage. The begging of my husband for me to seek professional help became chronic. It was then that I saw my first counselor, three decades after Daddy drove out of Sacramento and away from our family, as we had known it. It's as if we invited Trouble to move in with us. The circumstances surrounding Daddy's departure were devastating. The loss was profound. And yet, our family packed trauma and grief up in boxes to be stored and opened on another day. Except that we never did.

Trauma and grief will both resurface like beach balls held under the water as long as the one holding them has the strength to keep them submerged, out of sight. But eventually and assuredly, and often without warning, they will pop out of the water and whack the holder in the face, demanding their attention. It's inevitable.

> **Trauma and grief will both resurface like beach balls held under the water to keep them submerged, out of sight. Eventually they will pop up and whack the one holding them in the face, demanding their attention.**

My very first and new to me counselor was at least 20 years my senior. That fact, and her calm, confident demeanor was a comfort to me. It was no surprise that she started our first session together by asking why I was there. I honestly and ashamedly admitted that we were having some marriage problems and my husband often said I was controlling, but I couldn't see it, I didn't believe it. I went on to disclose that what bothered me most was that was exactly how my siblings and I saw our own mother. She was very controlling, and she couldn't see it, didn't believe it. But that was about the extent of my self-awareness. There wasn't any more. I simply wasn't self-aware and, although I didn't disclose that to my therapist, because quite frankly, I just didn't know it at the time, likely she did.

Although I don't remember a lot about that first session, I do remember that my counselor held her hands with fingers intertwined forcing both hands to tightly grip the other. I can still see her as she started releasing one finger in slow-motion-at-a-time and spread both hands with fingers wide, explaining that one hand was control, the other was fear. She then pressed her palms back together and locked all ten fingers again with an especially tight grip explaining that, if I would show up willing to talk about what I was afraid of, my words would require my hands to release their death grip one finger at a time. It was a powerful image as she slowly released her fingers on each hand, just one methodical finger at a time, explaining what I would soon discover. As I loosened the fingers of fear, the fingers of control would loosen themselves. She was right on the money.

Only Grace, No Grudges

I'm not blaming my mother. I have no desire to criticize who she was in her own Valley of Trouble with deep heartache and overwhelming disappointment. Nor do I blame nor judge my dad. They both have their own back stories and a lot of pain to go with it that created and supported their brokenness and ensuing decisions. I know they did the best job they could to get through life and be good parents. And in some ways, they were great parents. But the unhealthiness in any parent has a way of showing up as the same unhealthiness in any child, if not processed and released by that same child.

My mom's unhealthy need to control was passed down to me, but there was a significant difference between me and her. I had the privilege of seeking professional help. My mother did not. Professional help was taboo for a Christian woman living life in her era, it was different for me. I was responsible for seeking my own emotional health, and thanks to my husband and a few Christian therapists, I did. I'm grateful and hold no grudges but only grace for my mother and daddy, and those they remarried.

As I began to identify my fears in the office and presence of my first therapist, I found myself releasing those fears in the privacy of my own heart and home. I processed the heartache and pockets of trauma while leaning into a daily pause with Jesus, allowing me to catch my breath and, slowly but surely, my heart and my world began to release and transform that which no longer served me.

Control is often self-protection. I no longer had the need to vigilantly guard my wounded heart as it healed, and discouragement began to lift off my soul. It was then that I caught a glimpse of the pieces of my shattered heart being glued back together, one piece at a time (Psalm 147:3 TPT).

The Weight of the World

I did a double take of the elderly gentleman leaning against the pole at a bus stop I drove past. Bent over as if he could not bear his own weight for another minute. I wondered if it was the burden of his body or the load of the world on his shoulders? Hard to tell. His desperate roadside presence grabbed my attention, begging me to action. I nearly stopped to offer him a ride. Sadly, that doesn't work well anymore in this crazy world we call home. So, I prayed instead. Seems lame. It's not, but it felt that way as my heart screamed action, but my head spoke wisdom.

As I prayed and clutched the steering wheel, the burden clearly bearing down on his sagging shoulders and his hunched demeanor kept tugging at the compassionate edges of my heart. I drove on wondering. What was it that made the old man so worn out? Who drained life from his once potentially strapping frame? What cards had life dealt him requiring his tired self to lean on a pole? Was he headed home to a loved one's shoulder that he could cry on or at least rest his weary head? Was he headed someplace that felt nothing like home as he had once known?

Distracted, I made my way from traffic-light-to-traffic-light that lined the main drag of our quaint college town. My car was headed to the office. My mind was back at the bus stop. Life emptied from my stomach as a big knot began to replace peace.

Again, foreboding thoughts took my heart captive and the what-if plague took my mind hostage. What if things don't go well for my husband or our sons? What if one of them ends up like that old man? What if life disappoints them? I came to my senses for a split second and whispered to no one: It will. I know that. It's a given.

So, what if they can't handle the "it" life brings their way? What if the trouble they meet along their way leads them to shift away from faith or self-care? What if a secret sin takes them hostage like it did the leader in our community that we watched tumble from his high and respectable pedestal to a barren and lonely jail cell?

I was barraged with what- ifs about my husband. What if his Parkinson's Disease declines so severely that one day he can't walk or talk or eat? What if I must take care of him? What if I *can't* take care of him? What if it breaks my heart to watch Parkinson's wake up next to me each morning instead of Dave? What if we run out of money before we run out of time? What if he dies young and I'm left alone? What if I die young and he's left alone? What if something happens to me? What if I'm gone and Dave's health declines more? What if our sons or their wives have to take care of their dad? What if they *can't* take care of their dad? What if there's no one to take care of him? What if? What if? What if? The proverbial worry inquiry: What if?

Aware of the demise of my thoughts, I tried to sass back. Instead, my heart caught the sound of a faint melody within as I stepped onto an all too familiar imaginary dance floor and began the awkward dance with disappointment. In that moment, in my imagination, however, it didn't feel all that imaginary.

Disappointment wants to lead. We resist, but disappointment holds on tight and jerks us around the dance floor. The struggle is real. The image is not. No wonder Scripture tells us to take our thoughts captive to the obedience of Christ. (I Corinthians 2:5).

Obedience in Greek is the word, "hupakoe" and it holds the implication of "attentive hearkening."[7] Oh wow. That's instructive; I can tell my thoughts to "listen up and take notice" of Jesus and His ways. Jesus takes a lead role like that of a shepherd, a *good* Shepherd whose sheep know and trust they will be taken good care of. He leads and I follow, no longer trying to control or be the one in charge because He is, even when I don't know where He's leading, or understand what He's doing. The Good Shepherd offers his hand and asks: May I have this dance? That may not change the music, but it changes the dance, and calms the what-ifs within.

Ironically, the what-if questions were written in one of my journals some four or five years ago, and a good bit of what I worried about has become reality, other things have not. Regardless, the anecdote is the same, let the Good Shepherd lead the way. He is faithful in the valley of the shadow of death, so whether the what-ifs turn reality or not, we do not have to walk through them with fear. Jesus overcame the darkness so that we can be overshadowed by the light. Lean in to hear His voice and reflect on His ways. Take seriously that we are to be Christ *followers.*

When we lead and refuse to *be led,* discouragement is bound to visit us just like it did the elderly gentleman that God made sure I noticed that morning. In fact, *that's* what I saw leaning on the pole at the bus stop in the body of an old man: a weariness in facing another day that surely held new trouble without relief from yesterday's trouble. It's the helplessness of that once promising medical report, the conversation that goes nowhere, the once-a-month negative pregnancy test, the fresh start that delivers the same disappointing news as last time, and on and on it goes. The answer is no. Not now. And we wonder, will it ever be yes?

The old man offers us a picture of a precious life weighed down by trouble. It's a heavy weight, which is why Jesus invites us to lay it down, at any age or in any season of suffering. Lay it down, release it, surrender it, and yoke up with Him. There is another way. There is a fresh and encouraging perspective. The invitation of Jesus in Matthew 11 assures us that His burden is light, and His yoke is easy. More about that in chapter 10.

We follow Him and learn from His gentle and humble way. I know it's easier said than done, but I also know it can be done. Lay down the shattered pieces of your broken heart and life, your need to control, and your weary soul in His Presence, and breathe. The Holy Spirit is a Master at gathering them up for repair while you catch your breath in preparation for another day in your Valley of Trouble.

BREATHE DEEPLY

"When we breathe on purpose for as little as 5-minutes a day,
it calms our nervous system, boosts our energy, strengthens
our immune system and improves our health."
Stephanie Esser, Breath Coach[8]

INHALE

Read the passages below and reflect on or record
anything in them that catches your attention.

Psalm 46
John 20:19-22 (focus on verse 22)
Philippians 2:3-11
James 1:2-8

EXHALE

- Choose a verse, a sentence or just a phrase from one of the passages above.[9]
- Write it down on something you can post in your home, office or car, or at least carry with you.
- Meditate on its meaning; think about it again and again (and again!) over the course of your day/week.
- Read it in context.
- Read it in other Bible versions; the Amplified and Passion Translation are favorites.
- Look up the meaning of the words that you want to better understand.
- Memorize the verse or passage.
- Let the verse or phrase run around on the inside of you until it becomes your very own, part of your DNA.
- Consider personalizing it by inserting your name or praying it for yourself, someone else, or for a situation.

two
TRANSITION

"But we all, with unveiled face, continually seeing as in a mirror the glory of the Lord, are progressively being transformed into His image from one degree of glory to even more glory, which comes from the Lord, who is the Spirit."

2 CORINTHIANS 3:18 AMP

The length of our days are strung together by seasons of life with transition in-between. Transition means change. Change can be intimidating, frightening, overwhelming. Change can also be invigorating, helpful, and important. But one thing is for sure; change is inevitable whether a transition goes smoothly and is hardly noticeable or is excruciating and hardly bearable. As Jesus lovers and followers, we travel through life going from glory to glory, and in between the glory is a whole lot of transition and change marked by trouble and heartache.

Transition forces adjustment *in us* while requiring unexpected changes *around us*, often forcing us out of one season we may not feel ready to leave and into another we may not feel ready to embrace. When transitions pile up, we need a shelter where we can rest and catch our breath; a safe space or a safe person where we can grieve the loss of one season so that it's not too difficult to seize the next.

Some transitions, like a mother or father leaving the joy of parenting one stage of childhood to enter a new stage, or leaving one job for another can be intellectualized as natural, normal, maybe even joyful, meant to be adjusted to quickly. Others, like leaving married life to enter widowhood or single parenting or moving from a beloved home or city to put down roots in an unfamiliar place, takes time and carries with it the demand to process the burden of grief. Neither can be overlooked nor avoided but, instead, we move through it to clarify and own our new identity as change forces us out of the familiar and complacent, into a new thing God wants to do. Welcoming life as it is, not as it used to be nor as we long for it to be, is the path that leads us to fully champion and possess a new season. Our lives really would be dull and boring without change. The less we fight and resist it, the more we can see the gift that it is.

> When transitions pile up, we need a shelter where we can safely grieve the loss of one season so that it's not too difficult to seize the next.

We may be able to avoid change for a long stretch if we stay in the same house, in the same city, working the same job, living with the same person, keeping the same routine day-in-and-day-out. Maybe one can even pull off romancing sameness for a long, long time but, eventually, every single life will come face-to-face with transition on any given day, and changes will follow suit. Some change can be comforting and some stifling. So, whether you like variety and embrace change easily, or you resist it and prefer routine and having your ducks in a row, change will arrive with various forms of trouble in tow.

A Moving Truck Full of Change

It had been quite a day after waiting one full month for our belongings from Pennsylvania to arrive at our new home in Arizona. We were giddy when the trucking company called on Wednesday to say the moving van with our belongings would be arriving the next day between eight and noon. Thursday morning found me up unusually early with anticipation and abounding energy. After some quiet with my Bible and journal, a cup of coffee, and getting myself and the house ready, I headed out to the green space behind our new house to walk the dog. It was about 7:15 when I spotted the huge semi pulling into our development. I squinted enough to make out the writing on the door and it was, indeed, Crossing Country Van Lines. They were early! That moment was exciting and slightly unsettling – my husband and sister were fast asleep. I rushed Surfer (our dog) away from the bushes he was sniffing and scurried into the house, zipping into each bedroom as I breathlessly squawked at both Dave and Shirley to get up, get dressed and get outside! And with that, the move-in craze began.

The details about our first experience using a professional moving company gone wrong is insignificant because, in the end, most of our possessions arrived safe and sound. The small table and wrought iron shelf that came off the truck broken can be replaced or forgotten about. The dirt and grime on so many of our things can be cleaned off, and the half-opened boxes that looked like they may have been used as the football in a pickup game just didn't matter as we unpacked and broke them down to be recycled. When the day is done, our belongings are of lesser importance than anything else. The astronomical difference in the estimated quote and our payout was shocking but, as we settled in, that became a distant frustration. So, suffice it to say, like any move-in day, ours was packed full of stress. No pun intended.

Change often arrives in what feels like a moving truck that delivers and carries in familiar items that, quite frankly, just don't seem so familiar, really. Not when they deliver what we don't want, don't expect, and don't have any interest in keeping. Transition can feel more like damaged, dirty, half-opened items being dumped off than new, lustrous, more-useful items that hold potential for occupying our updated space, and life, with good.

Change plops us down among forced adjustments in a heap of self-pity, agonizing over what used to be, what looks ruined, feels like a mess, and needs to be cleaned up or repaired. When change arrives as a truckload, it overwhelms us, leaving frustration and a sense of overwhelm behind as the door closes when the movers head home. Transition erupts into an argument over what was promised but not delivered, and the forced adjustment dumps us among the boxes pining for what was.

It's challenging to embrace the new thing that God delivers, proving stressful at best. But God has a habit of sending truckloads of change while declaring that He's up to something new and good and promising. He presses us in those moments to stay curious so that we might be able to perceive the new, to welcome it as each box is unpacked (Isaiah 43:19).

Changes show up in our driveway over and over again, and often when we least expect the delivery truck! We can request (or beg!) that the load be taken to another address or come back on a better day, or we can choose to take a hard look at the old and the new, asking the Holy Spirit the significance of each upon their arrival!

Let's wake up the household, announce that the truck has arrived, and take a hard look at the change delivered. Welcome the new and the old knowing that the One who delivers is always up to something fresh and promising for our benefit. Take note and stay intrigued knowing that the truck has come for a reason that is bursting with newness of life.

The Sound of Heaven at Work

By late afternoon, I hit a wall and my sister insisted I lay down for a nap. I slept hard. It was one of those dead to the world, my body never even moved, kind of naps. But as I began to rouse about an hour later, I could faintly hear conversation and a slight scurrying of feet close by. I was just groggy enough that I wasn't quite sure what it was, but I had dreamed people were on our roof and woke up wondering why.

> **The sound of heaven is God at work while we're at rest.**

It was at that very moment I heard the Holy Spirit whisper to my spirit, "That is the sound of heaven; we work while you rest." I whispered back, "Is that you, Lord?" The Voice went on, "Yes, and that's how it's always meant to be in My kingdom; we work while you rest." I lingered on our bed for a brief moment in an attempt to let that sink in.

When God repeats Himself, I try to take note. What I heard from heaven certainly doesn't mean Jesus followers are to do nothing. More like God never meant for us to work to earn our salvation or strive to be a good Christian or figure out and try fix our problems by ourselves. Heaven carries out its will while we rest in the finished work of the cross. The Father, Son and Holy Spirit continuously work to redeem mankind, along with any given situation we're facing.

And all the while we rest in the finished (completed, debt-free) will of the Father and Jesus' death on the cross, for you and me (John 19:28-30). That's the glory Paul talked about.

As I left our bedroom and the comforts of our new cushy mattress, I was keenly aware that Holy Spirit was revealing a modern-day parable to my heart, and He wasn't quite done. When I rounded the corner to our bathroom that had literally been packed to the rafters with wardrobe and other boxes marked, "master bath" or "master bedroom" when I fell asleep, I now stood in a completely empty, box-free, rather large bathroom! I sluggishly wandered into our walk-in closet only to find our clothes on hangers, adding more glory to the picture!

My sweet sister was the main character in this personal, modern-day parable. Shirley worked while I slept. I know. Pretty amazing, right?! God used my sister's act of love in serving me to paint a beautiful picture of the

Holy Trio (trinity) literally working on my behalf while I literally rested on our bed.

This truth is such an unspeakable gift to all of us who call Jesus Savior and Lord. As we trust Father, Son and Holy Spirit and choose to cease from all of the commotion of our lives, we can rest in His care in-between the glory times where transition and change show up. There's a name for the place in-between for followers of Jesus best known as the Garden of Gethsemane; a space where transition is wrestled with, and surrender is beckoned.

The Garden in the Middle

In her book, *It's Not Supposed to Be This Way*,[10] Lysa TerKeurst unfolds the reality of our lives on earth lived between two gardens. There's the perfect Garden of Eden on one end (Genesis 3), a garden you and I have never been to, and there's the Garden of Eden restored on the other end (Revelation 21), a garden that you and I will one day gloriously enjoy in real time. The Garden of Eden became the platform for man's sin ushering in heartache, shame and disappointment on earth. The Garden of Eden restored will one day be the platform for all things to be made new, ushering in joy for all eternity. We live with the fallout of the first garden and the anticipation of the second.

When I first heard Lysa speak about living between these two gardens, it was a Holy Spirit mic drop moment for me as the revelation of a third garden came to mind: Gethsemane. I immediately took note that we often find ourselves in a garden between the first Eden and the last. There, we, like Jesus, spend the time it takes to surrender our will to the will of the Father. A place where we wrestle through any given assignment that we don't want, don't like, and don't think we can endure. Spellbound by its reality in our lives, it took me just a matter of days to create a lesson for the Bible study I was teaching and "The Garden in the Middle" was born.

The Garden in the Middle is where we see Jesus in all his humanity agonizing in a battle of His will while the disciples hit snooze. The weight of the world and its sin was literally settling on the shoulders of our soon to be Savior. That weight held indescribable distress for Jesus, Son of Man, as it pressed Him to the point of sweating drops of blood.

Gethsemane literally means, oil press.[11] Although you and I will never know the level of agony that Jesus endured in those moments in the garden, not to mention what it was like to be tortured and murdered on a cross, there is a slight hint of familiarity there. Paul Tripp in his Advent Devotional, *Come Let Us Adore Him*, describes this familiarity with Jesus this way, "God exposed Himself to all that we face in our terribly broken and dysfunctional world."[12] We'll never experience the weight of sin as Jesus did (Romans 6:10) and yet we have felt the heavy weight of brokenness in and around us, sometimes against us.

In the mystery of it all, you and I have moments when the pressure of life and the weight of the world can bear down on our shoulders, our heart, our relationships. The distress of life hits an all-time high when we feel the agony of heartache along with the overwhelming pressure to do what we must. And there we fight a battle between our will and God's (Luke 22:42). Elisabeth Elliot reminded her audience, of which I was often a part, that if we are going to pray that the Lord's will be done in our lives, then we must be willing to let our own will be *undone.* That's the hard part.

Jesus led his disciples to Gethsemane to pray immediately before His betrayal. You and I can take the pressure of our lives and pray to find strength for the unwanted assignment God is calling us to. If you were to read about Jesus in the Garden of Gethsemane in various translations of the Bible and pull phrases from all four gospel accounts describing His state of being in Gethsemane, you would see with even greater clarity the struggle and battle for His own will. But you don't have to gather that list, I did it for you. The eyewitnesses tell us that on that fateful night, Jesus was:

- deeply distressed.
- grieved/crushed with grief.
- battling intense feelings.
- depressed.
- troubled.
- exceedingly sad.
- overwhelmed with sorrow/anguish.
- struck with terror.
- in agony of mind.

We see the humanity of the Son of Man in Gethsemane possibly more distinctly than anywhere else in the Bible. In fact, Mark tells us that Jesus was *"so overcome with grief, that he threw himself face down on the ground"* *(Mark 14:35 TPT)*. Ever been there? It's that moment when we're wrestling with God about doing His will but wanting to hold on to ours, struggling and distraught. The Garden in the Middle is the space during a transition where we can pray and process with God until His will becomes our preference.

> **The Garden in the Middle is the space during a transition where we can pray and process with God until His will becomes our preference.**

Resurrection always follows Gethsemane. That's the glory! Resurrection brings new life to the deadness and hopelessness of our own heart. It's the newness, the possibilities, the miracles found in the glory. The opposite of the negativity of the world, the voices around us or those in us, screaming that because of this situation or that one, we're doomed. Our future is ruined. There is no help or hope for us. End of story. But that is never ever true for Jesus followers! Ever.

So, there's even more reason to run to the prayerful quiet of the struggle in the battle of wills where God's voice, God's will, and God's ways, can be heard and wrestled with so that we can come away with faith for the next step, and for tomorrow … and the next day … and the next … and the next …

> *"All the harsh realities of life aren't the end, but rather a temporary middle space. Not the place where we are meant to wallow and dwell. Rather the place through which we will have to learn to wrestle well which means acknowledging my feelings, but moving forward, letting my faith lead the way."*
> *— Lysa TerKeurst[13]*

The Garden in the Middle is the glory-to-glory journey of being transformed into the image of Jesus that Paul talks about. It's the place in-between our despondency at the cross on Good Friday and our dancing feet and singing heart that celebrates the resurrection on Easter Sunday (2 Corinthians 3:18).

The Garden in the Middle is the space called Saturday; the day in-between when our hearts can press pause to speculate the meaning of resurrection. The day in-between Good Friday and even Better Sunday. In-between John 19 and 20. In-between the darkest night and the brightest day. In-between believing and seeing. Saturday, the in-between day, where we often find ourselves transitioning and navigating unwanted changes between glory and glory.

When we're in the in-between, our hearts tend to sag with an uncomfortable fullness burdened by the overwhelming silence, haunting doubt, searing disappointment, unbearable grief, deferred hope, relentless despair, and so on. You fill in the blank.

The Garden in the Middle
is the space during a
transition where we can
pray and process
with God until
His will becomes our
preference.

On the day in-between, our heads bow low while our hearts slump even lower, and our countenance follows with haste. But on Saturday that sits in-between the cross and the resurrection, revelation comes rushing to our aide, bouncing up-and-down within us as it joyfully heralds the good news: Faith lives in the Saturdays of life! Faith lives in the in-between! Faith flourishes in between glory and glory and can thrive in transition and change! In between the darkness and the light. In-between the believing and the seeing. In-between despair and hope. In-between the desperate attempts and the quiet surrender *there is hope*. And that hope gives us just enough strength to take the next step into the unfamiliar, the new, the uncharted places God is calling us to.

Faith is inspired in the place in-between instructing us to tell our hearts to put on dancing shoes and begin to hum a melody of breakthrough and wonder, for Sunday's dawn is just about to burst forth, and celebration is soon in order.

Transitions don't exist permanently although, at times, they drag on and on. Change doesn't always show up in a moving truck, although it can pile up like a hamper full of dirty laundry. But the Garden in the Middle offers hope in our seasons of transition, giving purpose to the remodeling God is requiring of us.

> **Biblical hope promises an inheritance of glory that simply cannot be compared to a lifetime of suffering.**

It's in that place where we submit to the Father's will and begin to catch our breath again, even though potentially unbearable circumstances are still in front of us, looming over us. It's in that place in-between where we remind our hearts to hope again, knowing that a resurrection experience always follows a Gethsemane moment.

Resurrection literally means to stand up again and again... and again... and again... So, we go to the Garden in the Middle when disappointment turned discouragement is pressing hard on our shoulders because we believe that on the other side of our heartache, we can slowly stand up and walk forward. Not completely on our own, however. It's not about trying to be strong or religious in an attempt to earn brownie points with God. It's not about us working hard to figure things out. We submit our will and stand up by taking hold of the nail-scarred hands of Jesus who showed us the way out of the Garden in the Middle. We trust Him and His timing for the resurrection of what is dead in us, maybe around us, so that we can let go of what life is right now, or was back then, and fasten our hearts securely to what life can be, to a hopeful future. Although likely, not trouble-free. Very likely, in fact.

Biblical hope promises an inheritance of glory that simply cannot be compared to a lifetime of suffering. A hope that goes beyond the best of wishful thinking. It's that kind of hope that will always be the shift we desperately need in our seasons of transition, in order to catch our breath and march to the next peak of His glory.

BREATHE DEEPLY

"Inhale the future. Exhale the past."
— Author Unknown

INHALE

Read all of the verses below in The Passion Translation if you can.

Matthew 26:36–39
John 18:1
Romans 8:14-39
2 Corinthians 4:7–14
Philippians 3:7-14

EXHALE

- Choose a verse, a sentence or just a phrase from one of the passages above.[14]
- Write it down on something you can post in your home, office or car, or at least carry with you.
- Meditate on its meaning; think about it again and again (and again!) over the course of your day/week.
- Read it in context.
- Read it in other Bible versions; the Amplified and Passion Translation are favorites.
- Look up the meaning of the words that you want to better understand.
- Memorize the verse or passage.
- Let the verse or phrase run around on the inside of you until it becomes your very own, part of your DNA.
- Consider personalizing it by inserting your name, or praying it for yourself, someone else, or for a situation.

three
GRIEVED

> *"But as for me, I will look expectant for the Lord and with confidence in Him I will keep watch; I will wait (with confident expectation) for the God of my salvation. My God will hear me. Do not rejoice over me [amid my tragedies], O my enemy. Though I fall, I will rise; though I sit in the darkness [of distress] the Lord is a light for me!"*
>
> Micah 7:7-8 AMP

don't think I will ever forget the exact time, the exact day, nor the exact date when I tumbled into a valley of darkness: Tuesday, October 29th just after midnight is forever etched on my heart.

The darkness of that distressing moment convinced me that I might not ever rise again. The valley of the shadow of death engulfed me as a season of grief overcame my whole being. It was a season complete with long days, cold nights, and a barrenness of soul unlike other difficult times. In fact, it's fair to say it was treacherous. The necessary hibernation it demanded felt like a prison cell that closed in on my heart making it hard to catch my breath from the very moment Dave woke me from a sound sleep with the jarring news just a few minutes after 1:00 in the morning to tell me that she was gone.

Grief can be like that: jarring, shrill, grating, harsh on the soul. Grief, a natural and unavoidable response to loss. We know that grief is a natural response to losing someone or something significant. We know in our head that we should grieve, but we don't always give it credence in our behavior. Grieving can make us feel weak. God knew that. He sent Jesus clothed in humanity so that He could identify with our weakness, in or out of grief (Roman 8:3TPT). Jesus grieved.

Making Time for Intentional Lament

Jesus wept in His grief (John 11:1-35). The implications of the shortest verse in the Bible couldn't possibly indicate a gentle tear trickled down his Hallmark cheek. He wept. When someone weeps, they shed tears that may include sobbing, wailing, or heaving with sorrow. We can't know exactly how hard Jesus cried, only Mary, Martha and a few others were privy to that. We do know that He left the perfection of heaven where there is no sadness or dying and came to earth as a baby to be clothed in humanity where there is an abundance of sadness and dying. The Son of Man wept (John 1:14; Galatians 4:4-5). He felt what we feel. Like us, Jesus knows the despair of grief. Unlike Jesus, I had to learn to intentionally connect with my humanity instead of trying to be super-human by ignoring or denying my feelings. Brandie Mavrich, a dear sister with an anointed and prophetic voice in the body of Christ, explains it this way ...

"Too often, as Jesus followers, we hyper-spiritualize our lives in an attempt to make everything make sense in a spiritual way. We seek to get everything as a download from heaven which can be a disconnect from our humanity.

"Jesus, on the other hand, hyper-humanized the experience of life on earth. He left His place in glory to put on skin forever. He was born as a baby and died on a cross for every ounce of who we are.

"He is our sympathetic High Priest who is well-acquainted with every earthly experience, emotion, and response of ours on our journey here. Jesus became like us." - Brandie Mavrich

The Man of Sorrows bids us come to Him when we're weary and heavy burdened (Matthew 11:28). He welcomes every part of us: our anger, doubt, sadness, guilt, confusion, depression, and fear. He is aware of the emotions attached to our lamenting, and each is welcome in His Presence. There's no pressure to clean up and stop crying. Tears are a release and when we release what hurts, we can recover from the pain.

Grief is not a time for comparison. No two people will grieve the same, we are free to grieve in the way and for the duration that works best for our healing. Grief is not a destination so it can't be rushed. Grief is a process by where we come to understand that some measure of grief will accompany us for the rest of our lives.

Grief is part of life. Every single life on earth will grieve because every single life on earth ends in death, and we share life with one another. But grief isn't always attached to physical death. There is immeasurable loss in changing jobs, a child leaving home, miscarriage, divorce, chronic illness, moving, and more. Experiences that carry with them death of another kind. They, too, beg us to honor our need to process grief and make time for intentional lament.

In loss, we must accommodate grief. We cannot escape it even though it hurts. And for some, to say "it hurts" is a severe understatement. Loss is meant to hurt. Loss is painful and pain, whether in our body or our soul, begs for relief and healing. Therefore, we trust grief and choose to walk through its process. That's typically not a solo act. Most of us need some essence of community to process grief.

We must sit with the natural emotions of grief so that we can move through the natural process of grief into some form of new normal that we may even be convinced we don't want, didn't expect, and certainly would never choose. It hurts and, therefore, we often seek to avoid, deny, or suppress the pain, our grief.

When we avoid grief, we can expect it to show up later. Because it will. Grief always waits for you and me. It begs for attention until it gets attention. And when it knows we're ready, grief will typically hit us right between the eyes as a storm of emotion. It can be the song on the play list, the smell wafting by, the familiar scene, the nighttime dream, or anything else that brings back the memory of who or what was lost with a vengeance, and it catches us unaware. That's when we're forced to collect the effects of the storm when they come. Grief cannot be avoided, at least not forever. *To avoid grief is simply to postpone heartache and healing.*

When you and I deny our need to grieve, it makes us sick. Quite literally. Denial initiates illness in one way or another. It will show up as disease in our body, our soul, our relationships, our faith, or all the above. Denial is self-protection and natural when loss is sudden and unexpected; a safeguard when the loss doesn't feel real and while our heart catches up with its reality. It's the irreversible nature of loss that provokes us to deny reality. We just can't believe it. We don't want to believe it. But the loss is real, so we contest it in hopes it will somehow reverse itself and life can be what it was again. *To deny our need to grieve creates unresolved emotions that lead to illness of some kind, in some way, at some point.*

When we suppress grief, it numbs our emotions and stifles our senses. We can desensitize what we're feeling, but when we won't disclose our grief, the love, kindness and support that we desperately need from others won't penetrate the pain of our soul and may even go unnoticed. Although we have managed to protect ourselves from feeling or receiving pain, we also can't feel or receive the pleasant. Suppressing grief, swallowing tears, pushing emotions down, and refusing to express them, puts a shield around our heart that lets nothing out ... and nothing in. *To suppress grief is to numb our souls and keep life as it was meant to be enjoyed at bay.*

I once heard a man speak on grief who pointed out that the theology surrounding grief is hard. I agree. We have to reckon with the fact that, before the beginning of time, God knew that the person or the thing we lost would be taken from us. God knew we would grieve and that injustice would be part of our story, well-acquainted with the details. He allowed the loss. He is sovereign and all-powerful. He could have written a different script for your life and mine, but He didn't. It's hard theology.

Read the book of Job, a story that is more about, or at least as much about, the Sovereignty of God as it is the suffering of man. Namely, Job. We read Job and must agree with the man I heard speak all those years ago; the theology around grief is hard, at least with our limited earthly perspective.

But, beyond the difficult theology surrounding our suffering on earth is the perspective of heaven: the grief and heartache we feel now is temporary, it will not last forever. One day God will wipe every tear away for good, there will never again be death, sorrow, crying, or pain (Revelation 21:4). Revelation 21, near the end of the Bible, may be the most hopeful and glorious chapter of the entire Bible! It describes the intended end for those of us who follow Jesus and trust God's sovereignty in all things on earth, even loss and grief and sorrow.

When we trust the sovereignty of God and His bigger picture, His best plan, His purpose, it helps you and me to believe in a better ending to our right now grievous story.

In his book, *A Daily Devotional*, late pastor and author Ray Stedman's entry of September 26 includes a quote from someone that he doesn't identify. This unnamed friend refers to heaven as "a place of 'no more' – no more death, no more sorrow, parting, pain, tears, evil – all are no more!" In our grief, we can encourage ourselves by imagining that soon coming day when the heartache of loss and dying will be no more. No more being or being left out. No more fear or feeling unsafe. No more worry or anxiety.

No more trouble or heartache. No more the need to be strong, brave, resilient … you fill in the blank.

What is it that you long for on that soon coming day? What can your heart celebrate *now* that will be "no more" *then*? The internal celebration, if you will, can hold and sustain you and me in our grief in a way that nothing else will. It's the very reason we can grieve, but not as those without hope (1Thessalonian 4:13).

Seasons of suffering can be transformed when we see our pain through the lens of eternity. There's always more to God's story than what meets the eye. But the accuser, the enemy of our soul, the evil one, the thief, is likened to a hungry, roaring lion whose aim is to devour his victims. He is ever attempting to take the circumstances of our life to steal our joy, our peace, our faith, and so much more (John 10:10; 1 Peter 5:8).

> **Seasons of suffering can be transformed when we see our pain through the lens of eternity.**

It is always to our advantage to take the time to notice, acknowledge, and pray about the attack on our soul from the enemy of God and man, clarifying our perspective on what is happening to us and around us. We are a people in a battle that started in the Garden of Eden. The scene in the first garden reveals the reality that all that God loves, the enemy hates. All that God is, the enemy is not. God loves His creation and His children. Satan hates us. God is generous. Satan is a thief. God unifies. Satan isolates. God is truth. Satan is deceit. God is grace. Satan is condemnation. God's creation, His children… you and me… are the target of the Father's deep love and good plans. We are also the target of the enemy's evil schemes and deceitful strategies.

Always and forever true, while we're on earth, and although understanding that may not relieve our grief, it can instruct us and give purpose to our suffering, making a little more sense out of what we're going through on earth. And one day, there will be no more battles, no more threats from the evil one, no more accusations, no more war within our soul. There will be no more sudden and unexpected tragedy striking us as it did Job.

The loss and deep grief of the Old Testament character, Job, his whole story, in fact, has much to offer us in ours. The first chapter of Job's book, where his familiar story begins, allows its readers to be privy to a conversation between Satan (a name that literally means "accuser") and God, about Job. We can read the chilling dialogue, and we must realize that Job was totally unaware of the words exchanged at the throne of God that day. Only the angels were within earshot of what the accuser and God spoke about (Job 1:6-13).

> *"There's a scene in heaven, unseen to Job and others on earth,*
> *but absolutely real nonetheless. The story of Job can really only*
> *be properly understood by taking into account what happened in*
> *heaven, and by having more than an earthly perspective."*
> *— David Guzik[15]*

Sudden and Unexpected

When my friend-like-a-sister died suddenly and unexpectedly, other significant things in my life died with her. In fact, when Jess stepped into heaven, I stepped into a graveyard that annihilated plans and dreams with her, fun and laughter, friendship, and sisterhood full of phone calls, shopping, double dates with our hubbies, beach vacations, birthday celebrations, game nights, prayer and comfort, home decorating, and so much more. Loss upon loss surrounded the permanent absence of my dear friend-like-a-sister.

None of us grieve a person's absence alone, although that is profound. We grieve all that they brought to the table that enriched our soul and added meaning to our days. We grieve all that was and was going to be with them. Saying goodbye to someone on earth stops our world in its tracks, seeking to convince us that we may never feel normal again, and the darkness may always be a threat. In fact, to know grief is to be acquainted with despair.

Jess and I raised our kids together in their early years. Our husbands were very close friends. We stayed in touch for two plus decades while living on opposite sides of the country. We talked often of growing old together and had plans to be the cute little old ladies at the retirement center who made others smile and each other laugh. So, to say that we were ecstatic to be living just a few miles apart again, after Dave and I relocated, would be an understatement. And to say that I felt her untimely death like an electric shock to my system inside and out, an even greater understatement.

> **None of us grieve a person's absence alone. We grieve all that they brought to the table that enriched our soul and gave added meaning to our days.**

Jess sat straight up in bed on that fateful October night long before the sun had a chance to shine. It was the jolt of her body and her facial contortions that alerted her husband, who thought she was dreaming, before it registered that something was wrong. Terribly wrong. It was only a matter of minutes before my dear friend gasped her last breath on earth only to inhale her first breath in eternity, while her devoted husband waited for the paramedics to arrive. That moment for Jess was what all Jesus lovers and followers live for: entrance into His Presence, forever and ever. A triumphant moment for Jess with a sense of glory that earth dwellers simply cannot comprehend. And at that very same moment, less than a year after Dave and I moved to live close to Randy and Jess, life turned into an unsettling whirlwind for those of us who loved her.

Surely nothing could have prepared any of us for the agony of her homegoing. There were no signs, no warnings, nothing in the physical realm that would point to Jess' untimely death in her late 50s. The whirlwind of an unforeseen and sudden death delivers unmatched shock and chaos.

You, too, may have memory of having been taken hostage by an unexpected and shocking death of someone or something you loved and desperately wanted to stay. Death, whether completely unexpected or the result of a long illness, is a disturbance to one's body, soul and spirit that is like no other. In his book, *A Grief Observed,* C.S. Lewis describes the death of a loved one as "an amputation."[16] Ironically, years before reading Lewis' book, I often described living on earth without my late brother as an attempt at living without one of my limbs. I used to say it felt like someone cut my arm off and I had to learn how to live without it.

The loss of my brother was different than the loss of my friend. It forced us to grieve slowly for over a decade, losing Ron a little bit at a time. Grief can linger and its delivery can be methodical, or it can arrive as a blow that forces its way in suddenly. Both bring loss, and loss is hard. Slow grief gives the gift of time, while sudden grief is a thief of time. Sudden grief demands we face our loss while slow grief can deceive and deny and hide our loss. Even from us. Slow grief wearies the soul, sudden grief overwhelms the soul.

Slow grief is like a constant drip trickling from a leaky faucet that beats, beats, beats on one's resilience every day for a long time, threatening to drain every ounce of life left within. Sudden grief is like a fire hydrant bursting with a tremendous force that knocks one down, threating to drown. Slow grief is incredibly hard. Sudden grief is incredibly hard. Neither is easier nor harder than the other, they are just different.

Three short weeks after Jess went to heaven, while Dave and I were still in the trance of deep sorrow, we suddenly and unexpectedly had to say goodbye to our beloved 8-year-old dog. If you're a dog lover, you get it. Regardless, those two losses catapulted my heart into darkness: a cold bitter winter of sorts.

The profound loss became a catalyst for years of multiple losses that I personally found challenging to fully grieve. After all, how does one grieve the daily loss of a spouse with a degenerate disease while they're sitting right next to you on the couch? How does one calculate the weight of losses trailered across the country from Central Pennsylvania to the desert of Arizona? Add in pounds and pounds of loss after saying goodbye to a beloved house, church and community, where our children were loved and grew for 20+ years. There's far too much loss to calculate of the closer-than-sister kinds of friends left behind in the Keystone State... a church dearly loved that just so happened to be my employer... a ministry job never taken for granted, and so many precious daughters of my heart who were under my ministry care.

You have your list, too, and are likely acquainted with a pile of adjustments alongside the loss of the familiar, the predictable, the names and faces of acquaintances, the locations well-known ... and so much more.

Insurmountable losses can keep us down and threaten to never let us rise again. How does one adjust to the loss of an ex-spouse who lives across town? What about the loss of a child who won't respond to the text, the call, or the holiday invitation? Or the loss of identity in retirement? A job loss or a move to a new community can be packed full of grief. What about the loss of a dream hijacked by something unforeseen, health and abilities taken away by an injury or disease or aging? How on earth do we respond to the loss of those proportions and grieve our way back to good health and a steady heart in our new normal? I wasn't quite sure either.

A Winter Season

Grief upon grief upon compounded grief can lead one into a winter season. A dark, bitter cold one that catches you or me by surprise and badgers our bewildered soul. The theology of it is eminently hard. And the God of that theology is eminently good. He is not the author of confusion; but is the same good and faithful God in the dark bitter cold season just as He is in the bright warm season of rejoicing.

We become different. He remains the same (Hebrews 13:8). He hears you and me, and He helps us rise from the ashes of grief. He alone is a light for us. We can look expectantly to Him and, with confidence, keep watch, believing He *will* show up, He *will* speak into the darkness, and He *will* *not* leave us alone in the valley of the shadow of death.

My winter season suspended the darkness as I sat through days, weeks and months that were mostly a blur. Grief surrounded me like fog and sedated life to slow motion, leaving me numb and mute. I leaned into the sorrow while fighting it off at the same time. I saw a grief counselor weekly and was painfully honest about my journey with my dear confessional friends. I would cry out to God when I had the energy, declaring by faith that I still believed. I reminded myself that He alone could soothe my tender soul and guide me to the other side of the profound sadness, severe disappointment, heavy heartache, dazed confusion, and overwhelming grief.

We believe what we say, so choose your self-talk wisely when you're hurting. I often cried out, "God – help my unbelief!" And most importantly, I showed up. I just showed up. Every single sad morning after sad morning I showed up and settled into my heaven on earth chair while I waited. I would read the Word of God and listen until He spoke from the pages of my Bible or into the ears of my heart. In the deep sorrow and emotional weakness, I had to choose over and over to stay instead of running or hiding. Stay in His Presence and feel the crushing weight of grief with Him before standing again to laboriously press toward a new normal that I couldn't see and, quite frankly, didn't want. One small, unsteady step at a time.

And when I showed up, I had to talk to my heart, even when it was barely a whisper, and I could hardly believe what I was saying. I told myself about the One who comes close when a heart is breaking (Psalm 34:18). I reminded myself that Jesus was also acquainted with grief (Isaiah 53:3). Whatever the Word of God said, I said to my heart. And amid the self-talk, I felt the weight of the words that the enemy of my soul, the father of lies, whispered to convince me that my God is distant and dismisses my heartache and pain (John 8:44). I had to remember, especially in my grief, that the enemy is a liar. Because the truth of the matter of grief is that There. Is. Nothing. Further. From. The. Truth.

God is close but the enemy never ever speaks the truth about anything, particularly about God's character. I told my heart that I would not fall for his lies because I knew that my future depended on me rejecting each one of them. I declared over and over and over again that I am a beloved daughter of the King living on earth while engaging with another kingdom; the kingdom of heaven that is at hand (Luke 17:20-21; Romans 14:17). As a kingdom girl (just another name for a Jesus follower), I take my cues from the written word of God and the Spirit of God. Any other source can potentially be deadly when grief is a constant companion.

Wrapped around those days of acute grief, my daily manna (bread) came primarily from the Psalms. As a kingdom girl, I had to persistently consider that my spirit cannot stay alive on bread in my kitchen alone. My soul actually can be resurrected so that I can catch my breath when I consume the words that comes out of the mouth of God (Matthew 4:4), even when I'm grieving. Especially when I'm grieving.

Some mornings it was just a bread crumb that brought relief, one verse or just a phrase within a verse was often enough to help me catch my breath and stand up again. And the comfort of Psalm 34:18 had been familiar manna for me. My eyes and head had read it and received it time and time again, but in the darkness of grief, it became a fresh piece of bread that fed my ravenous, lamenting soul. It's a word for the grieving and bears reading in various versions of the Bible.

- *"If your heart is broken, you'll find God right there; if you're kicked in the gut, he'll help you catch your breath." (The Message)*
- *"When someone is hurting or brokenhearted, the Eternal moves in close and revives them in their pain." (The Voice)*
- *"The Lord is near to those who have a broken heart and saves such as have a contrite spirit." (NKJV)*
- *"The Lord is close to all whose heart is crushed by pain, and he is always ready to restore the repentant one." (TPT)*

The keywords in this short verse begged me to new discoveries in the original Hebrew from the Strong's Concordance Bible app:

The Lord: literally, Jehovah; the Hebrew name for God that means Self-Existent One; the Eternal One[17]

near/nigh: in place, as kindred, in time, at hand, allied, as neighbor or kin, kinsfolk/kinsman[18]

broken: literally or figuratively to burst, to break down or off into pieces, crushed, hurt, torn, destroyed; saves: to open wide or set free, by implication to be unsafe[19]

contrite: crushed literally to powder, destroyed[20]

So, I took great liberties to personalize and paraphrase the words of the Psalmist in Psalm 34:18, according to the Hebrew word meanings:

The Eternal One comes near and sits with me in my grief. My Self-Existent God shows up like a relative or an ally in a time of trouble, just to be there with me. My God comes near when it feels like my heart might burst into a million pieces and the crushing heartache threatens to destroy me. Jehovah is my safe place. He arrives on my doorstep to be close so that He can open wide this tight and suffocating space of grief that makes me feel like a prisoner of my own heartache. He comes near with freedom on His heart and mind longing to release me from the overwhelming sadness and soul longing for life as it was.

The Eternal One, my Self-Existent God, is close when it feels like my heart has been crushed to powder and cannot be repaired. He is not distant in times like these. He does not dismiss my pain, nor did it take Him by surprise. He is not watching me from heaven's throne far off and distant. No, He is sitting smack in the middle of the grief and confusion with me.

He walks through the long, hard days with me helping me cope and process the sorrow. And He will be with me every step of this difficult way and right into the new normal. My God, the Eternal One, is closer than a brother or a friend, and that is my comfort.

As kingdom people, may we never accuse God of being far away, ignoring us, or taking our pain and loss lightly. The King of this kingdom is the One who bears the weight of grief with us and walks the journey of grief beside us. After all, He is the Man of Sorrows who is acquainted with grief (Isaiah 53:3). That kingdom reality alone can calm and instruct our souls.

God is close when it feels like our hearts have been crushed beyond repair, convinced we're in it alone. God is not distant. He does not dismiss our pain, nor did what happened to us take Him by surprise. He is not simply watching our lives unfold from a distance but is sitting in our grief *with us* and walking *next to us* as we put one foot in front of the other toward a new normal that we never wanted, but that He planned before the beginning of time.

Sleeping Through Your Storm

There's a familiar story in the Gospels that tells of a turbulent storm that whipped up in a moment's notice on a lake in Galilee while Jesus and his guys were boating to the other side. In the account, we find the Son of Man seemingly oblivious to the threat of the thrashing wind and sloshing waves. Jesus is unaltered, unafraid, unaffected by the storm that is terrorizing the disciples. And he is sleeping, mind you!

"Out of nowhere, a vicious storm blew over the sea.
Waves were lapping up over the boat, threatening to overtake it!
Yet Jesus was asleep."
Matthew 8:23 The Voice

Storms on the water and storms in life put you and me in a precarious position. The enemy seeks to convince us that storms are terrifying, and fear is our only recourse. Our soul convinces us that we have permission to worry and every right to panic and persuades us to give into the inner-trembling, and let faith slip overboard.

So, we hang on for dear life while begging God to stop the storm already! We may even silently accuse Him of not being concerned about our fate at all, as the disciples did, wondering if Jesus prefers His sleep over our rescue. But here's the thing; for Jesus, trusting the Father is just like breathing. He and the Father are One. Jesus trusted the Father eminently, and still does. Therefore, His propensity is to trust, in this case, sleep, instead of panic. His response is always an opposite way … an opposite perspective … an opposite turn of events, than ours. His ways are better than yours, better than mine, and usually beyond our awareness. His thoughts are higher than ours (Isaiah 55:8-9). Even in the storm of grief.

"Jesus was sleeping in the storm not because He was exhausted
but because the world He dwells in has no storms. Jesus was
able to release into the natural external environment what He
was already experiencing on the inside. Our lives were always
meant to be lived inside out, not the other way around."
- Bill Johnson, internet/social media

We may not be able to get out of the boat and off the water but, just like He did for the disciples, Jesus can calm the storm, and we can position ourselves to stay in that calmness and catch our breath. Jesus didn't sleep in denial of reality, He was simply trusting His Father, the Maker of heaven and earth. Jesus was resting in the Father's care. Totally at peace, confident that all would be well beyond the raging storm. Jesus knew that water splashing over the sides of the boat wasn't any more of a threat than it was an indication that God the Father didn't care or didn't notice.

The storm always presents itself as a vicious enemy. The Savior always presents Himself as a Victorious Rescuer. It is no different in the storm of our loss and lament. We, too, can sleep through our storms, not to deny nor escape reality, but because we know we cannot always hush the storm, only our response to it. And there, in the raging storms of life, our fear is empowered not by looking at the storm, but our faith is empowered by listening to His words. We can sleep through our storms because we know the One who calms the storm also calms the frightening threat in us. We sleep because the Maker of heaven and earth commands vicious storms to cease with an impeccable choice of timing. We can sleep through our storms because the Father never does.

> **We cannot always hush the storm, only our response to it.**

Positioning ourselves in calmness happens when we declare the promise of grief: We can never "lose" God and He will never leave nor forsake us (Hebrews 3:5). Even in our deepest moments of grief, God remains. And in that truth, our lamenting hearts take solace over and over again, letting its promise settle within us as we catch our breath. As our lungs fill up with fresh air, the eyes of our heart can look toward the horizon to catch a glimmer of light from our new normal, seeking to usher in fresh hope and a measure of relief for our hurting, grieving heart.

BREATHE DEEPLY

"Shallow breathers poison themselves."
– Paul Bragg[21]

INHALE

John 11:1-35
1 Thessalonians 4:13-18
1 Peter 5:5-11
Revelation 21:1-7

EXHALE

- Choose a verse, a sentence or just a phrase from one of the passages above.[22]
- Write it down on something you can post in your home, office or car, or at least carry with you.
- Meditate on its meaning; think about it again and again (and again!) over the course of your day/week.
- Read it in context.
- Read it in other Bible versions; the Amplified and Passion Translation are favorites.
- Look up the meaning of the words that you want to better understand.
- Memorize the verse or passage.
- Let the verse or phrase run around on the inside of you until it becomes your very own, part of your DNA.
- Consider personalizing it by inserting your name, or praying it for yourself, someone else, or for a situation.

four
WAITING

"Let Your [steadfast] lovingkindness, O Lord, be upon us,
in proportion as we have hoped in You."

PSALM 33:22 AMP

The waiting ... and waiting ... and waiting ... of something hoped for or life to return to normal can mark any given circumstance hopeless, because we feel helpless. It's when we don't know what to do, the situation doesn't change, and the prayers go unanswered, that we lose our grip on control and begin to apprehend the truth that we were never in control in the first place. A harsh and hard reality to swallow.

The waiting rooms of life are not where we like to hang. It's there that our very real, very comforting sense of control is stripped

> **Where there is no mystery, there is no need for faith.**

away, leaving us longing for someone or something we can't have and can't get back. It's a yearning that shakes us to our core with a profound sadness as we try to navigate the trouble or heartache staring us down. And yet, it's less about the sadness and more about the longing for what was and never will be again.

Waiting fosters a desperation to bring back the familiar; the person or the situation we long for. But in the waiting, there is always a measure of mystery, and the weight of that mystery grows heavy as we become increasingly uncomfortable in the confusion that a long season of waiting can bring. There we come to terms with what will never return to the way it was and are forced to face the mystery of that harsh reality. But where there is no mystery, there is no need for faith.

Faith is the way of the cross. Following Jesus requires faith and without it there is no pleasing God (Hebrews 11:1, 6). So, we trust in our times of waiting, even though pregnant with unanswered questions and seemingly forgotten prayers. Seasons of waiting hold out an invitation to lean into trusting Jesus while we wait; and wait while we trust Him. It's in that tension where we discover it really is viable to live with trouble and heartache while still believing in a good tomorrow. Faith is not the absence of doubt, it is the presence of hope.

When This Is Over

Dave and I had a lesson to learn during a long season of waiting. We literally had to train ourselves to refrain from saying, "When this is over, we'll do that" or "when this is over, we'll go there" or "when this is over, we'll ..." We had to fight to stay in the present moments and acknowledge that *this* wasn't over. The more we let those phrases slip from our lips, the more disappointment and discouragement filled our days. Every time the reality that *this,* in fact, wasn't over, it smacked us in the face, and we were disheartened all over again. It broke down our resolve and sucked courage out of our perseverance. It drained hope from our veins and out of our hearts. We would get up in the morning bright and cheery about the new day, but the minute Dave got up and had pain, or I lost my patience with Parkinson's, or... reality would hit, and we had to face that we were still in *this,* and that very reality would knock us down again.

Don't get me wrong, God's mercies were (are!) absolutely new every morning, but we had to stop telling ourselves that life would be good *when this was over* or *when that changed.* Those are deadly statements that keep you and me from living in the present and trusting God with what is making us weary in the waiting.

God is good even when life isn't. He alone knows when we're about to turn a corner and run head on into victory. In the meantime, He is able to fortify our souls to wait some more, and sometimes He may even require us to sing while we wait. God often whispers to my heart that I can sing my way out of any given difficulty and go beyond my discouragement induced by waiting for Him to move.

I felt a little self-conscious doing it at first, but I had no audience, so I relented. During that long season of waiting and learning lessons, I would often mutter brief melodies declaring the Lord's power and majesty in an effort to realign my expectation to His good intentions, and His ability to deliver me while I waited on Him. I never wrote any of the lyrics to those random melodies down, although I wish I had. But they often went something like this, set to no particular tune:

"Lord, you are great, and your heart is for me!
Lord, you are faithful, and your mind is on me!
Jesus you are good, and You alone are my way out!
I trust you and honor your faithfulness.
You steady my heart and are my firm foundation.
You are good! You are powerful! You are God.
You are *my* God, and my life is in your hands.
No worry will befall me, no fear will overwhelm me, no darkness will overtake me as I wait for Your goodness and glory to come.
You are my Strong Tower and the Strength of my heart ..."

Where there is no mystery, there is no need for *faith.*

You get the picture. Simple, random, made-up melodies meandering through my mind until they found their way onto my lips, increasing my faith and building up my courage as God healed me from the inside-out, while I waited on Him. All done in the privacy of my own heart and home. Thank goodness!

Songs of deliverance often marked the lives of those in the kingdom of heaven on earth. Saul found relief from a tormenting spirit when King David played his stringed instrument (I Samuel 16:14-23). Music therapy of sorts. And what about the story of King Jehoshaphat leading a choir to march in front of the army singing praise to the Lord (2 Chronicles 20:1-30)? You may remember that as the choir sang, the people of Judah watched their enemies fall and tasted victory in a battle that should have brought defeat.

In the New Testament, Paul and Silas begin to pray and sing in their jail cell around midnight which was followed by an earthquake that suddenly shook their prison doors open, and their chains loose (Acts 16:16-36). But these bold Jesus followers chose to stay in prison and, as a result, the jailer and his entire family came into the kingdom that very night.

When God's people wait on Him and lift their voice in praise, He often moves! Songs of deliverance can come on the heels of breakthrough, or they can usher it in. Just ask the Israelites who encountered a miracle from heaven on the shores of the Red Sea. The Israelites had just left the comfort of their homes in Egypt where they lived a life of slavery. But nonetheless, it was a life they knew all too well. Generations of Hebrews had endured the bondage of life in Egypt and resisted being pushed out of their comfort zone. They left all that was familiar, although oppressive, to follow Moses to a land unknown that God had promised them. However, unbeknownst to them, their journey *out* of bondage was about to lead them *into* a long season of wandering in the wilderness for 40 long and wearisome years. Talk about a long season of waiting! But they were still in Egypt as they began their exodus and one of their first stops was on the shores of the Red Sea. They had Pharaoh and his army breathing down their necks, and the deep sea in front of them with no way around it. The situation was classic trouble; there's just no way out of this! The Israelites were terrified and surely felt helpless because it looked hopeless!

I've had seasons of hanging out on the shores of my own red sea. I bet you have too. My guess is that, like me, you prefer the mountain top. We want a perpetual season of life on cruise control where all is well, peaceful, hassle-free. But it's in those moments on the edge of the water, when the situation feels hopeless and prayers seem to go unheard, that the power of the Living God shows up and does the most amazing things.

And in that exact moment in Jewish history, Moses says something puzzling to God's people and, in fact, potentially frustrating: *"Do not be afraid. Stand firm and you will see the deliverance the LORD will bring. The Egyptians you see today you will never see again. The LORD will fight for you; you need only to be still" (Exodus 14:13).*

Maybe the Israelites expected that kind of faith from their leader. Regardless, the story takes another perplexing turn when God immediately reprimands Moses, *"Why are you crying out to me? Tell the Israelites to move on. Raise your staff and stretch out your hand over the sea to divide the water so that the Israelites can go through the sea on dry ground" (Exodus 14:14).*

Wait. Did God just say what I think He did? Move on, as in, walk right into the waters of the Red Sea? In the original script God said, *"Tell the Israelites to go forward."* Go forward? Seriously? My guess is, in that moment, they preferred Mo's instruction to "stand still" over God's to walk into the water. Jehovah said in essence: Don't just stand there, this is not the time for that. Go forward. So, with the water in front of them, and their enemies behind them, where were they supposed to go?

Nonetheless, Moses said, "Never mind, God says go so, let's go!" Moses stretched his rod over the sea which sent the waters rolling backward and upward creating a wall that invited the Israelites to safely walk to the other side of the shore. It didn't take long for the pursuing Egyptians to get caught in the rush of waves crashing back to the seabed. And the enemies of the Israelites were no more, just as Moses had said.

I don't know about you, but I can't even get my head around the reality that the Israelites survived that day as recorded in Exodus 14 and 15. So, was it like a tsunami that lasted long enough for God's men, women and children to run across the bed of the sea just in time for it to come crashing down on the Egyptians? Or did the Egyptians drown in shallow water, which I guess would be a miracle all its own? It's hard to say. The Red Sea is deep but also has extensive shallow sea shelves, but Scripture says they walked through a wall of water on either side. So, although we can't know exactly, the miraculous nature of that day is sure and recorded in history.

Can you imagine experiencing this in real time? What was it like to walk (or run) on dry ground in the depths of the sea with a wall of water piled high on both sides? The image terrifies me, and I'm certain it was far more frightening than my 2nd grade students watching my red Jello red sea in the 9x13 baking dish being pulled back by their teacher with "invisible" Saranwrap. Smile. (I made Red Sea Jello every year in an effort to make this Old Testament account come alive for children. I have a strong hunch that I failed miserably to bring the reality of the story to life for my students.)

This was real sea water. The Israelites were being pursued by real and unreasonable enemies. Moses had a real rod that had unreal powers; supernatural, miracle-working powers because of the word of the Lord. And the Israelites walked on the bottom of a real sea on real land. Dry land, nonetheless. They lived a real miracle. They weren't just listening to the story being told at church on Sunday morning. The Israelites encountered the power of the Living God in real time! Scripture tells us after this experience, they feared the Lord and put their trust in Him, and in Moses, on that very real and unusual day. You should read the story again for yourself. It's truly remarkable and awe-inspiring, although admittedly incredibly hard to imagine!

When we find ourselves standing on our own shores of uncertainty waiting on God, there are miracles planned for us. When we've got God's promise in front of us, and the enemy gaining ground behind us, shaking in our boots as we watch our situation go from perplexing-to-threatening-to-frightening-to-overwhelming-to-hopeless, there are Red Sea miracles waiting for us! It's the place where we uncover a gold mine of revelation and application.

Speaking of which, let's hop over the choppy waters of the Red Sea to see that, as Israel walked through the dry ground, they began to sing. The first thing out of their mouths when the miraculous show ended was a song … to the Lord, about the Lord. God birthed a song in His people after years and years of slavery, 400 to be exact, and moved them toward freedom and out of bondage.

That gives new meaning to a waiting season. There surely were no songs of rejoicing in Egypt for centuries. The Israelites only hummed to the beat of serious heartache, exhausting misery, and unrelenting toil and bondage. But when they came into the wilderness and onto the shores of the Red Sea, they took a front row seat to the power of God. And when they experienced it, they broke out in song.

That's the way of the kingdom of heaven on earth; lives are met with great challenges that require great faith. God brings great deliverance evoking great praise! God delivered the Israelites that day quickly and miraculously, which isn't always the exact scenario playing out in our lives. We have tasted and seen that the Lord values waiting and hoping in Him and shows up in our seasons of waiting in unexpected ways, but the Red Sea is an even more powerful picture than most of us can imagine.

You may know that the Israelites traveled in the desert for 40 years on their way to a land promised to them. This was a trip that should have taken about 11 days (Deuteronomy 1:2). Pause and ponder that as it relates to waiting on God, being patient and letting the Lord work out the details of the challenging situation staring you down.

There was no song before that day. No rejoicing, no freedom, no joy in Egypt, only bondage and control and heartache and toil from sun-up to sun-down. They were a people enslaved and oppressed by Pharaoh. God's miraculous provision at the Red Sea changed their experience and their identity. This was the beginning of their wandering and waiting on the Lord, and their Warrior showed up over and over again during those long 40 years!

Sing and shout your way out of what you're going through, praise Him while you wait. And when you can't find a song within, find some worship music and hum along until a song rises up within your soul. No matter what the situation weighing heavy on your heart and always in your mind, no matter how bad it looks or how discouraged you may feel as you wait, your God is a Warrior. He is for you, and not against you. He has victory on His heart that belongs to you, so go ahead and make some music while you wait!

Buried Underneath the Pile

I found myself waking up to severe angst over the transition Dave and I had been living in after moving from Pennsylvania to Arizona. It seemed as if change showed up like a moving van every single morning to unload another pile of confusion on the doorstep of our hearts. I simply could not catch my breath as I got buried underneath the new piles of uncharted territory.

You know. You've been under your own piles gasping for air. It was during a personal Sabbath time when the Holy Spirit pressed me to cease from writing what was on my heart and switch to writing what was on His. Here's a peek into my journal that day, written as God in the first person, which is how He so often encourages and instructs my soul: "You've been taking care of yourself for so, so long. You've often felt alone and weary, which is different than tired and weary.

Feeling alone carries with it…

- an emotional weight that feels heavy
- an emptiness that feels anxious
- burdens for tomorrow that feel frightening
- a false sense of responsibility that feels real

"I am your Sabbath-Rest; the place you can stop, lay it all down, lean on Me, and breathe while you wait, and more change arrives. I invite you to rest. I will solve the problems with you. I will shush you and love you while you sit still. I will sing over you with joy as you receive my tender loving care. Change chokes.

"Waiting with no vision for tomorrow suffocates. I am your safe place in the waiting, and feeling safe always lets you breathe, and then breathe some more. Stay with Me awhile so you can catch your breath before getting back up to face what's next.

"Sherilyn — I am your Sabbath rest. Come to Me, I wait with you. Bring your soul that's ever so weary from feeling alone and believing it's all up to you. Yoke with me. Learn from me. Breathe and breathe again even while you wait. I am safe. You are home, child, for I am your Sabbath-Rest."

Habitually Holding Space

When was the last time you enjoyed a Sabbath? You may be wondering if I mean on Sunday as in, did you go to church, go out to lunch, and take a nap? Maybe. That may be your true Sabbath. But then again, maybe not.

I had the pleasure of working for a church, as paid staff, for many years, so Sunday wasn't my Sabbath during that time. Monday was, and for decades it was Monday morning as my schedule could barely squeeze those few hours in for "ceasing from labor."

As Jesus followers, our sabbath practices can be more than resting in the sense of a Sunday kind of Sabbath that we church-goers know of. That's good, but there's more. Sabbath is not just rest from working hard, although rest on Sabbath is good. Really good. But I'm not sure God rested from exhaustion after He created the heavens and earth (Genesis 2:2-3).

The Hebrew word for rest literally means, "to cease, put an end to" which carries the implication of intentionally putting an end to regular activity"[23] Practicing Sabbath is to cease from work and accomplishing, much like God did at the beginning of time. He modeled taking a Sabbath when He stopped working on the seventh day of creation. He did not rest to restore His strength. He is strength. He did not stop because He was fatigued. He never grows weary or tired. God simply stopped creating. He had completed His work and on the seventh day He enjoyed that work and rested.

The Hebrew word "sabat" literally means, to cease.[24] Shabat carries the implication of celebration, so we can accurately read Genesis 2:2 as: God blessed the seventh day and set it apart from other days as holy because on that day He stopped creating and celebrated the work He had done. Such a Sabbath celebration becomes rest for one's souls.

We notice in Genesis 2 that the work of God, the creation of the world, was finished on day seven with no definitive mention of evening or morning like the other six days. Could it be that there was no keeping track of time on that blessed day of rest and enjoyment? Could it be that the Sabbath isn't about a timeframe but about stopping, and more specifically, stopping to enjoy? It's in that celebration of delight where you and I will find rest for our weary souls that are required to wait.

> **Personal Sabbath will soften the damaging effects of discouragement that come from long seasons of waiting.**

Habitually holding space for Sabbath isn't about discipline, although it will take discipline to turn our attention away from the usual work we do, the distractions we're used to, habits that fit into our daily schedules, and more. But ultimately, observing a Sabbath is about delight. Taking delight in the One who holds out rest for our weary souls that are required to endure waiting, and then expected to wait some more.

Sabbath is pausing to take pleasure in spending time with the One who has our lives under control, even when they feel out of control. In fact, especially so. Sabbath calms the distress of waiting and helps us trust in His sovereignty for what we wait and long for. Personal Sabbath will soften the damaging effects of discouragement that come from long seasons of waiting in our lives.

No matter the cause for the weariness of your heavy heart, no matter how much you long for what was, or hope against what might be, holding space for a personal Sabbath offers the soothing and refreshing you and I so desperately need.

Honoring a personal Sabbath is less about the discipline of extended, intentional and uninterrupted time to rest, and more about the pleasure of extended, intentional and uninterrupted time to revisit and engage with the Father's love, the words of Jesus, and the comfort and guidance of the Holy Spirit. A personal Sabbath can be an hour ... a morning or an afternoon ... it can be a whole day. It can be Sunday or Wednesday or Thursday. The day and time aren't the important things. Encountering Jesus and resting in Him who was able to say, "It is finished!" is what matters.

His work on the cross made a way for you and me to have life on earth and for all eternity. Jesus satisfied the requirements of the law and became the Sabbath-Rest for our souls (Matthew 5:17-20). He alone is the treasure while we wait. He alone makes observing a Sabbath a delight while we wait, and He alone softens and soothes the damaging effects of weariness in long seasons of waiting. So, we set aside time with Him while we wait, and there we find deep rest for our souls ravaged by the trouble and influenced by the changes in our lives, captivated by Him all over again.

Rest in the words He speaks to your heart during Sabbath. They will sound like yours and, if they don't contradict scripture, trust they are from Him. Jesus is "the Word" (John 1:1-5) so, clearly, He always has something to say over and over again. He hasn't stopped speaking, and He longs to speak specifically *to* you, *about* you and the season you find yourself in. Listen and believe you've heard Him.

If you aren't sure if what you've heard is from the Lord, ask a trusted friend, your Bible Study teacher, or a pastor who hears His voice. God is no respecter of persons. He speaks to me and countless others; He will speak to you. I promise that His voice will encourage and instruct your heart too, and you'll never be the same.

Get still and be quiet. Listen, and you'll hear His voice. Start with just an hour. It can seem daunting if you've never done such a thing, but use the resource provided at the end of this chapter: *One Hour with God*. Let it guide you and help you practice being with God for just one hour. I'm confident it will leave you wanting another hour and then another and another and …. and when the hour is up, you'll notice that you are able to catch your breath and press on, even while you wait.

BREATHE DEEPLY

"A common symptom of anxiety and other forms of stress can be shallow and erratic breathing patterns, which reduce the oxygen levels in our brains, exacerbating the very agitation that triggered our shallow breathing in the first place. Breathing deeply reverses this vicious cycle, helping us think more clearly, slowing our hearts, reducing our cortisol levels, and calming our mental chatter."
– Pete Greig, How to Pray; A Simple Guide for Normal People[25]

INHALE

Isaiah 30
Isaiah 40:27-31
Hebrews 4 (focus your attention on verses 14-16)
1 Corinthians 10

EXHALE

- Choose a verse, a sentence or just a phrase from one of the passages above.[26]
- Write it down on something you can post in your home, office or car, or at least carry with you.
- Meditate on its meaning; think about it again and again (and again!) over the course of your day/week.
- Read it in context.
- Read it in other Bible versions; the Amplified and Passion Translation are favorites.
- Look up the meaning of the words that you want to better understand.
- Memorize the verse or passage.
- Let the verse or phrase run around on the inside of you until it becomes your very own, part of your DNA.
- Consider personalizing it by inserting your name, or praying it for yourself, someone else, or for a situation.

ONE HOUR WITH GOD

"The best way to start praying is actually to stop praying.
To pause. To be still. To put down your prayer list and
surrender your own personal agenda. To stop talking at God
long enough to focus on the wonder of who He actually is.
To 'be still before the Lord and wait patiently on Him.'"
- Pete Greig, How to Pray: A Simple Guide for Normal People[27]

FOCUS YOUR MIND ON GOD THE FATHER, JESUS THE SON AND THE HOLY SPIRIT

- Close your eyes and relax for a few minutes.
  Ask God to quiet your mind and speak to your heart.
- Read a Psalm out loud.
- Praise God for the things mentioned about Him in the Psalm you read.
  Thank Him for who He is.

REPENT AND SURRENDER YOUR WILL

- Surrender your will to God's control.
  Lay down trying to be your own boss, god, a fixer of all things, etc.
- Sit quietly with the Holy Spirit and ask Him to reveal any sin, hurtful thoughts or words, rebellion of any kind within you.
- Briefly ponder your sin. Only long enough to own it.
  Thank Jesus you are forgiven because of the cross.
  If necessary, pray about apologizing to someone you may have hurt or offended.

EXPRESS YOUR GRATITUDE

- Write down or name out loud a few specific things or people you're thankful for, and why.
- Thank God for the gift of each one and reflect on ways He has provided for and helped you.
- Thank the Lord for answers to your prayers, for help from the Holy Spirit, for the Written Word of God and its effect on you, and those you love.

HUMBLE AND SOFTEN YOUR HEART

- Bring your burdens to mind and imagine laying them out in front of you.
- Ponder or journal about any fears or lies attached to each burden that may be trying to control or speak over you.
- Sit with each burden as you release it to into God's care, even if you must do it every day for 365 days.

SETTLE YOUR HEART AND DECLARE HIS WORTH

- Read or work on the book of the Bible or Bible Study you're currently going through.
- Journal about what's on your heart, what in His Word is speaking to you and the related prayers you want to see answered.
  Try sitting with a blank page of your journal open so you can write down what you hear the Holy Spirit speak to your heart.
  You'll know it's Him if it's encouraging, doesn't contradict Scripture, and points your attention to Jesus and His ways.
- Memorize or meditate on a verse you read today remind yourself who God is and what He wants to do in you and for you.

SET YOUR HEART FOR THE DAY

- Use your imagination to visualize the truth He seems to be working in you or your circumstances.
- End by reading the Psalm you started with today.
  Declare who God will be to you regarding who the Psalm says He is.
  > Today when I feel overwhelmed by that person or that circumstance, I will trust that God will be my refuge, He is safe, and I run to Him to feel safe. He will be my wisdom and the strength of my heart. He is not overwhelmed like I am.
- Ask God to give you peace today. Sit quietly for a few more minutes before entering (or rushing into) your day or the next place of responsibility.

*Think of this as a template. There is *so much more* you can do, pray, reflect on in your hour with God, but start here, and tell God you want more. More of Him, more faith, more revelation, etc.

> *"Do not be anxious or worried about anything, but in everything [every circumstance and situation] by prayer and petition with thanksgiving, continue to make your [specific] requests known to God. And the peace of God [that peace which reassures the heart, that peace] which transcends all understanding, [that peace which] stands guard over your hearts and your minds in Christ Jesus [is yours]."*
> *Philippians 4:6-7 AMP*

five
UNCERTAIN

*"God is our refuge and strength, a very present help in trouble.
Therefore, we will not fear ..."*

PSALM 46:1-2A

There is one word that both lay people and professionals use to describe Parkinson's Disease: *slow.*

Slow moving. Slow processing. Slow responding. Slow talking. And more. "Slow" began to mark my husband's body in his early 50s and, together, we unknowingly rolled into a Valley of Trouble that was foreign, but matched the diagnosis, as every day began to play out in slow motion.

A few years beyond the slow symptoms catching my attention, Dave was officially diagnosed with early on-set Parkinson's. He was 54. It is ironic that, up until that time, both of us could have been described by using the antonym for slow. Dave and I lived *fast*. He worked fast and I talked fast. He got ready fast, and I drove fast. We ate fast and cleaned up fast. We fought fast and forgave fast. And we often argued about him walking so fast that I couldn't keep up even though I tried, and I tried hard!

Facing the reality that our fast, furious, and full life, as we knew it, had come to a slow halt, better known as Parkinson's Disease, was a discouraging fact. However, not immediately. That process was slow too. When a new way of life moves into your house and begins to turn everything upside down, you don't really have time to give much attention to how unsettled your soul is feeling. But it is.

I can certainly tell you about the times I painfully watched my athletic, well-coordinated, fast-moving husband begin to struggle just to get up from the couch, or out of the car, or to button his shirt, or tackle going upstairs, but I don't recall that sense of coming undone harassing me. Not early on anyway. Maybe I just didn't notice. It's hard to say.

Unexpected changes have a way of moving in and taking over before you recognize that your dwelling is a tent in a valley called Trouble. But honestly, I couldn't catch my breath long enough to feel uneasy or disturbed. The changes that Parkinson's delivered on our doorstep came at the speed of light for both Dave and me. There wasn't time to ask God the five whys and a how question when I had to handle the finances for the first time in 25+ years of marriage, or while concern and confusion over what was happening to my husband took up so much mental real estate.

Navigating a balancing act between working and being a helpful wife-turned-advocate, while letting my husband maintain his independence and make decisions, robbed me of any resemblance of discretionary time for adjusting. So, I pressed on. I didn't even know to look for space to grieve as we began to let go of a future we had both dreamed of, when daily life was overshadowed by the challenges of PD. I was busy, busy, busy researching the disease, organizing a plethora of new medications, and getting acquainted with new ways of relating to Dave and navigating life. My new normal consisted of days packed with PD interruptions and the ramifications of sleep disturbance, and on and on the growing symptomatic list went.

And then there was denial. It can serve you for a while, but it also tends to leave a trail of poor health, brain fog, and messy relationships. But soon enough it happens; reality smacks you upside the head when you least expect it to, want it to. Eventually it always does. The changes chase you down and wrestle you to the floor, forcing you to face your new reality. That carpet-gazing low point for me took place in Terminal 2, Gate 31, at the San Diego International Airport.

More Questions Than Answers

I stood there nauseous as I wondered where Dave could possibly be and why he wasn't answering his phone as pre-boarding for our eastbound flight was well underway. I anxiously waited and frantically scanned the wide corridor leading to our gate. His faint, slow gait soon came into sight. I watched him nearly limp toward me, looking atypically flustered as he tried to navigate his luggage and backpack, both seemingly so heavy. I wondered if someone had played a cruel joke on him and filled them with rocks. Heavy ones.

Reality showed up the precise minute I sighted him and right there at Gate 32, I was shoved into a valley, and as I tumbled down, my heart grew faint. An avalanche of deep concern seemed to beat down on me with force. Literally. My knees felt like they might buckle, my bottom lip quivered, and surely the blood drained from my face as I heard myself whisper under my breath, in a Parkinson's kind of slowness, "Dear. Jesus. What. Is. Happening. To. My. Husband?"

Dave seemed almost unrecognizable to me that day. I was accustomed to a very handsome, extremely athletic, extraordinarily strong and in-charge man who had taken good care of our sons and me for the previous two-and-a-half decades. Where was *that* husband? When did his big, gorgeous smile disappear? What had zapped him of strength and left him seemingly unable to carry a backpack without struggle? It was truly perplexing … and frightening. But thank God, I was able to stay somewhat composed even as I frantically wiped each tear that tried to escape and trickle down my face in an effort to conceal my concern from Dave and the crowd of boarding passengers surrounding us.

A new reality was delivered that day. A sad one. Although the San Diego International Airport held many happy memories for us with a handful of sad goodbyes, it morphed into a valley of trouble on that particular day, casting us into a season of uncertainty.

Trouble comes in the front door, the back door, the windows, and the garage on any given day, in every home. Typically unannounced, it arrives without warning; but even if there is some kind of lead-up event, it's a challenge to face Trouble head on. Instead, we attempt to boss it around, speaking sternly to no one in particular, "Not this time, buddy! Not now! Not again!" All in hopes that the unwanted intruder will head right back out the same door it came in.

Trouble shows up in the text, the email, the argument, the call from the doctor. It can catch us unaware at the office, the family gathering, church, home, in the car, while vacationing, or on the phone. It can be delivered by a friend, a husband, a wife, a child, a neighbor, or the devil himself. It comes in the form of regret, a damaging thought, hurtful words, a miscommunication … or some unexpected stark reality that publicly smacks us in the face at an airport. You get it. Who doesn't?

Trouble is no respecter of persons and knocks on everybody's door. Trouble can be as daily as an unruly toddler or as overwhelming as an unexpected health crisis or that of a million other scenarios in between. Trouble has one goal in mind: To discourage its victim and escort them into a season of uncertainty.

And sometimes Trouble can show up at the airport dressed up as Parkinson's disease.

Posture Matters

"By faith Abraham obeyed when he was called to go out to the place which he would receive as an inheritance. And he went out, not knowing where he was going, By faith he dwelt in the land of promise as in a foreign country … for he waited for the city which has foundations. Whose builder and maker is God."
Hebrews 11:10

Abraham of the Old Testament was in a season of uncertainty when his changed perspective changed the game and, in his case, altered the journey for him. Don't you love Bible verses that can change the game? Hebrews 11:10 is one of those. Abraham packed up his family and belongings and left the most familiar place he knew to journey to a place he didn't know one single bit. All because God directed him to. Hebrews 11:10 is referring to his obedience to his God during that season.

Like Abraham, we, too, can obey God and move forward in faith during seasons of uncertainty as we keep our attention on that unseen city, our final destination, and off what we just can't figure out. Uncertainty can feel like the earth beneath us is literally shaking and shifting, making it a challenge to stand up straight or find our balance. It leaves our spirits feeling small, hunched, nearly crumpled.

Parkinson's does that to one's body as it significantly impacts posture. Dave's experience was no different, I know, I had a front row seat. It's as if the PD Task Master presses down hard on the top of the head and pushes with even greater force on the back of the knees, making one's stature appear small, hunched, nearly crumpled. Posture matters, literally and figuratively. PD warriors know that, and their care providers encourage them to be more intentional about standing up straight and, in fact, using a mirror to check their posture throughout the day.

That's good advice for all of us; check the posture of our spirit, especially when life is uncertain. Our spirit, the place where we commune and house the Living God. The reality of a future unknown pregnant with unpredictability makes or breaks us in a season of uncertainty. All the more reason to find a mirror and check our posture, the posture of our spirit.

> **Posturing ourselves to stay vulnerable, in the process, and openhanded, can change the game in a season of uncertainty.**

The posture of one's body affects balance, and good posture enhances their activity and protects their movements. The good posture of one's spirit can enhance their decision-making and protect personal boundaries. Both affect one's mindset and emotional stamina. Posture matters … in our body and in our soul. Posturing ourselves to stay vulnerable, stay in the process, and stay openhanded, can change the game in a season of uncertainty.

Stay Vulnerable

Have you noticed how we prefer the rules of life and relationships to be precisely defined, black and white, good and bad, especially "we" religious people? There's a pseudo sense of comfort in our avoid-vulnerability-at-all-costs bent. We humans like to be comfortable, not vulnerable. But it's vulnerability that can inspire faith that pushes you and me beyond our comfort. If you're a comfort-seeker, don't skip to the next chapter, hear me out.

Staying vulnerable– honest open and real with ourselves, with God and with trusted others– will increase our faith giving us a greater capacity to trust God. Let me explain. I have the pleasure of being a part of a confessional community,[28] if three constitutes a community. We'll call it a confessional triad. In a confessional community, one can be gut-wrenchingly honest about disappointment, anger, heartache and more. The honest storytelling is for the sake of "being soothed, seen, safe and secure" by others *so that* we can encounter the same thing with God. The gut-wrenching honesty is not for the sake of staying in the raw emotion or desires expressed, there's no badge given for staying stuck. But those in a confessional community value the practice of being vulnerable and honoring personal integrity by not hiding but instead taking off masks, and being real.

In my confessional community, we "confess" our reality, the thoughts and feelings about the situations of our lives past and present, the things we might otherwise keep secret from the world and maybe even from ourselves. In our triad we "confess" *with* one another, not *to* one another; being with someone in confession is vastly different than confessing to them, or at them. My two confessional friends and I disagree sometimes, we give push back, all for the sake of each person being vulnerable, no longer hiding.

> *"Our deepest desire as humans is to be known — to be*
> *seen, soothed, made to feel safe, and secure."*
> *— Dr. Curt Thompson, M.D., The Soul of Desire*[29]

In this community of three, I've experienced the power of vulnerability to increase and deepen my faith. For instance, on any given day I might confess, admit to Becky and JoAnn, that I'm responding to Pete[30] unkindly, being impatient, or overreacting to PD and admitting the truth, postures my heart to discover what's really underneath those reactions ... overreactions.

Recently, that very confession and the help of my two trusted friends provided an unveiling of the overwhelm mingled with fear I was feeling. Both were disguised and hiding under the apparel of anger, frustration, and intolerance. As my friends helped me peel back the layers of my heart, the fear about what the uncertain future with PD would be for Dave and me came to the surface, to my attention. Interestingly, after processing in this beloved community of three, that discovery and admission dislodged the fear and worry, the overwhelm and grief within, opening space for faith. In facing my feelings and my reality head on, it became clear what was igniting my overreactions and the fear of an unknown future, and I was finally able to let go, release the emotional responses that were no longer a benefit to me, nor Pete.

As Christians, we can be afraid of truth. That's tragic, as it's the very truth we deny or hide from that positions our hearts to break free from whatever weighs us down and keeps us stuck (John 8:31-32). Speaking the truth isn't wrong, it's *how* we speak truth that can be. Speaking the truth and listening through a lens of His grace is healthy and helpful, not to mention necessary. Truth can be hard to talk about. And truth can be the very thing that sets us free! Is it any wonder the enemy wants us to deny or confuse the truth? Freedom is not on his mind for us; bondage is.

As my trusted friends soothed me while I confessed and processed, the need to more fully trust God with my future came to the surface. God, like my friends, is with me in the fear of the unknown. He knows my future. He's in my future. He's preparing and calling me there. His goodness is there. Each time I'm vulnerable, my faith is enlarged. To be vulnerable is to be seen as we are, not as we clean up.

> **To be vulnerable is to be seen as we are, not as we clean up.**

Choosing vulnerability deepens our faith because it calls out fear, anger, FOMO, jealousy, loneliness, etc. Faith pleases God and threatens the enemy. He tries from every angle to keep us stuck in our thoughts or feelings. Vulnerability is always about release, letting go, moving forward.

Staying in a posture of vulnerability releases faith to believe in what we cannot see. At least not yet. At the heart of vulnerability is risk, and at the heart of faith is the same. Faith will always require you and me to take a risk. Ultimately, as Jesus followers, we must answer the question over and over again: Will we risk our future on God's words and faithfulness even though we don't know what He's up to nor why?

> *"Vulnerability is uncertainty, risk, and emotional exposure.*
> *Vulnerability is not weakness;*
> *it's our most accurate measure of courage."*
> *— Brene Brown[31]*

Faith, like posture, matters. It's impossible to please God without faith (Hebrews 11:6). It attracts the attention of heaven and changes our perspective. Faith has nothing to do with effort that tries to muster it up in hopes God will be pleased with us. That's religion. The posture that takes the risk of being vulnerable opens the door for us to take a similar risk of faith. It's in that very posture that we are set free to walk through life without being significantly affected by what we see around us (2 Corinthians 5:7) so that we can journey through life trusting God instead of reacting to what's happening. The problem we often face is that we want to have faith while having understanding. But that's not faith. There is no faith where there is no mystery.

Understanding begs for some kind of explanation and assurance. Faith chooses to leave the mystery with God who sees all and knows all. Wisdom reminds us that leaning on our own understanding has limitations, but acknowledging God and His good will does not.

> *"Faith is built on trust, not understanding."*
> *— Christine Cain[32]*

Stay in the Process

Posturing our hearts to wait in the process of the good work Jesus is doing in and around us builds our confidence (Philippians 1:6). Waiting is hard, but process is good. They go hand-in-hand. Staying in the process gives purpose to our suffering in uncertain seasons and meaning for the circumstances we endure, but don't understand. Our desire to control and figure things out both take our focus off the work within us that is *still* happening. When we focus on the circumstances that are uncertain, it centers our attention on what we think we can fix or figure out. And uncertain circumstances can cause us to grow weary quickly. It's the unknown, the unresolved, the unexpected, that weighs us down.

God has a good work He's doing that you and I often don't see. There is an intentional plan that heaven is working on behind the scenes in our families, our businesses, our churches and ministries, and more. That is true even in a season of uncertainty and, in fact, maybe especially so in such a season. We just aren't always privy to what God is up to. But we can rest assured that there are no random assignments. Stay in the process when things feel uncertain and trust the intentions of heaven for your life and your growth, and His influence on those around you.

Seeing the Finished Project

Dave and I recently renovated our small condo in Southern California that we now call home. The tenants before us made the small living space, well, unlivable. It was filthy and damaged, in desperate need of professional attention. So, we hired a contractor because of his track record for doing exceptional work, both structurally and aesthetically. We signed a contract because of his affordability and promised adherence to stay within our budget.

All through our many months long project, I lovingly referred to him as Demolition Doug, and on any given day, Dave or I could walk into our condo and become immediately discouraged by what we saw … or didn't see. But Demolition Doug never seemed discouraged. He had a blueprint and was working the plan step-by-step, day-by-day. Doug knew it would be a long process. We could trust His expertise and his history with previous clients. He was confident in his work. He was always proceeding according to knowledge and experience. He was reliable and precise. So even though it often looked to us like the project was unfinished (it was!), we could wait in the process, trusting his expertise and plan.

Sure enough, a day came when we walked into our beautiful, *finished* little home. God is always doing something good. It's who He is (Mark 10:18). Jesus is doing a good work in us and for us no matter how things look in the moment. That's the reality we let inform our uncertainty. When we can only see the mess, we can trust in the One who has a plan and is working on it while we wait.

> *"So we are convinced that every detail of our lives is*
> *continually woven together for good, for we are his lovers*
> *who have been called to fulfill his designed purpose."*
> *Romans 8:28 The Voice*

This is a promise based on God's character. He is always working on something good in and for His children. We panic when it looks like there's no plan, or one that's been set aside and isn't looking the way we thought it would. We must carefully and intentionally choose our self-talk in those moments and remind ourselves that God always has a good plan whether it's for our earthly journey or our permanent lives in heaven.

Romans 8:28 is a sigh of relief kind of promise. When you and I focus on that truth, we can let go of trying to figure things out, fix or control them, because God has all things figured out, planned out for that matter. He has all things under His compassionate control even when life isn't kind but, instead, is unsettling.

> *"I'm confident that the Creator, who has begun such a*
> *good work among you, will not stop in mid-design but*
> *will keep perfecting you until the day Jesus the Anointed,*
> *our Liberating King, returns to redeem the world."*
> *Philippians 1:6 The Voice*

God doesn't have a track record for stopping in mid-design. He's not going to head out in the middle of any given project! We put our trust in Christ for salvation, make a conscious decision to be devoted to Him as we take up our cross every day and follow Him, and all the while, He is busy working on good things in us and for us. At that moment, in the uncertain season and for all eternity, His Son works in and around us.

He's for us and not against us. So, in seasons of uncertainty when life feels unstable, unpredictable, maybe even unfair, we choose a posture that can stay vulnerable, stay in the process …. and stay openhanded.

Stay Openhanded

You and I resist hardship and yet, we will endure it repeatedly. We can worry and fret our way through uncertainty, or we can pray our way through. And I don't mean we beg God through it (although I've tried!), but we ask in simple child-like faith and wait, leaving our hands open and praying with intentionality.

In any given season of uncertainty, prayer must take front and center on our calendars. Such a season will schedule a time, keep a Bible close by, maybe a journal, and always a verse to pray and declare over people and situations being prayed for.

You and I often spend a lot of time thinking and talking about our problems, and those of our friends and family, but in a season of uncertainty, talking and listening to God about those same people and situations is where the power lies, the change we long for.

Worry lacks authority and competence to help. Openhanded prayer is the posture of receiving. It's a dialogue, not a monologue. Open hands is the gesture of receiving from heaven. We can't give to others what we haven't received. God reveals himself to a soft heart. A hard heart bears pride, bitterness, offense, anger, unforgiveness, stubbornness, doubt, and unbelief. A soft heart and open hands will turn up the volume on the Voice of heaven making what the Holy Spirit wants to say to us clear.

> **Open hands is the gesture of receiving from heaven.**

"Be persistent and devoted in prayer, being alert and focused
in your prayer life with an attitude of thanksgiving."
Colossians 4:2 AMP

To devote ourselves to prayer is to continue praying, to press into prayer instead of fretting about the things that concern us, and there we can settle into the peace God promises (Philippians 4:6-7). Intentional prayer is full of gratitude, even in a time of suffering and uncertainty.

The word "thankful" in the New Testament is the Greek word, "eucharistos" where we get our English word, eucharist.[33] Participating in the eucharist offers someone a moment to be deeply thankful for the sacrifice Jesus made on the cross for them personally, not just for the world. He shed his blood *for them*. He gave up His life, His rights, His longings and wishes to do the Father's will, and to die so that you and I might have life on earth and be adopted into the Father's family.

This powerful, and biblical word, eucharistos, is imperative for keeping a posture of open hands; it literally means "grateful language."[34] A thankful heart opens the hands of one who comes to fully embrace that God is the One who gives and takes away and, in either scenario, we can raise our voice and say: Blessed be the name of the Lord (Job 1:21).

> *"Once I become thankful about something, it*
> *is no longer in the enemy's hands."*
> *— Bill Johnson, internet sermon/social media*

Eucharistos, grateful language, is important all through life, but vital in a time of uncertainty when fear and weariness make us susceptible to the evil one. Maintaining a posture of open hands, spilling over with thankfulness, will transform a season of uncertainty from frantic control to undisturbed contentedness. Staying in a posture with open hands shifts the focus from what we don't have and long for to what we can celebrate and be thankful for!

Standing with closed fists is a posture of fear; curling our fingers around what we can't control, don't understand, the things and people we think we can't live without. Standing with open hands is a posture of prayer; not only speaking but also listening to the Maker of heaven and earth; a sure way to catch our breath and let our hearts settle even when our circumstances are marked by an unknown future and feel unsure.

Using grateful language with ourselves, others, and with God, is a sure way to keep our souls from becoming even more self-reliant or consumed with anxiety in a season of uncertainty.

BREATHE DEEPLY

"Stooped posture reduces your ability to take deep breaths."
– parkinsons.org

INHALE

Psalm 131

Psalm 139

Colossians 3:1-17

Hebrews 11

EXHALE

- Choose a verse, a sentence or just a phrase from one of the passages above.[35]
- Write it down on something you can post in your home, office or car, or at least carry with you.
- Meditate on its meaning; think about it again and again (and again!) over the course of your day/week.
- Read it in context.
- Read it in other Bible versions; the Amplified and Passion Translation are favorites.
- Look up the meaning of the words that you want to better understand.
- Memorize the verse or passage.
- Let the verse or phrase run around on the inside of you until it becomes your very own, part of your DNA.
- Consider personalizing it by inserting your name, or praying it for yourself, someone else, or for a situation.

six
DISCOURAGED

"Though we experience every kind of pressure, we are not crushed. At times, we don't know what to do, but quitting is not an option. We are persecuted by others, but God has not forsaken us. We may be knocked down, but not out."

2 CORINTHIANS 4:8–9 TPT

When Dave and I met, we had a lot of things going for us. We were older and we knew what we wanted in a life partner. Sort of. We both loved the Lord, children, the beach, all things family, and had nearly identical values. We had a drive for maintaining a good work ethic. We loved our families of origin and, in fact, grew to love each other's families of origin. We were both independent. *Very* independent.

Although broken and in need of some soul healing when we said, "I do," we had a good marriage. We had differences of interest while being much the same in significant matters about how to do life. I love girlfriends and laughing, going to the theatre, and walking. I'm up at the crack of dawn and can burn the midnight oil. Dave loves dirt bikes and Harleys, a lot of alone time, and baseball. He's reserved and always early to bed and early to rise. At least before Parkinson's. We gave each other plenty of space to enjoy what mattered to us and loved our independence.

Life Changes

Early on with his PD diagnosis, we could enjoy our separateness as Parkison's slowly moved in with us. In fact, the first five years we were nearly able to ignore the disease to a certain degree. Eventually that changed. Dave started coming home regularly from the job he loved as a middle school health and physical education teacher, making comments I had never heard in our 30+ years of marriage. Comments like: "I'm exhausted, I don't know how much longer I can keep doing this, I was so tired at work today, I had to stop and sit on a ball bucket on my way to the gym from the soccer fields."

As his discomfort grew, so did my concern. His daily reflections were out of character for my never-wanting-to-complain-ever-grateful husband. The string of comments turned chronic, and, with them, life began to change, be it ever so slowly. Classic overtone for PD.

The morning that we sat together on the bottom step of our stairs so that I could help Dave put on his shoes and socks was one I will never forget. He was soon off to work nearly dragging his backpack, tired before the day had even begun. I watched his jeep drive out of view on Bayberry Drive as tears clouded my sight and, before I knew it, I was sobbing, aware I was losing the man I loved so much and had known to be a certain way for so long. That reality settled on my heart with a thud.

Discouragement doesn't have to have the last word.

Deep Brain What?

In my search for an alternate treatment for Parkinson's, I discovered a surgery called DBS: Deep Brain Stimulation. My insatiable need to know more began around the time Dave stepped into forced retirement. Not by the people he worked with, but by the disease he lived with. The research indicated that Dave was a likely candidate for DBS, so I set out to find just the right surgeon and just the right medical facility for surgery. Holy Spirit and I did our research and, after eliminating several places for reasons such as too far from home with no one close by, no longer taking our insurance, DBS being one of a hundred surgeries performed weekly and more, we landed on a Scripps Clinic in Southern California. It checked all the boxes. It was close to our sons and my extended family. We had a place to stay for the potential six-month post-surgery recovery.

The surgeon at this particular hospital performs DBS on brains nearly every single day, all day long. DBS surgery was his specialty. And a team of five medical professionals had to unanimously agree that Dave was indeed a good candidate. So, with his team and by God's amazing grace and sure favor, Dave was evaluated in January 2018 and underwent surgery the following July.

A New Lease on Life

We discovered that Dave's surgeon needs his patients to perform a few tasks during surgery so the wires can be accurately placed deep into the brain. Therefore, patients are required to be awake during DBS surgery. Typically, a patient is encouraged to bring something they love into the operating room. Things like an instrument to play, yarn to knit or crochet, a canvas to paint, you get the picture. Dave asked Dr. Moore if he could bring his Harley to rev it up or a baseball bat to swing, but he received an emphatic, "Um. No!" Dave's sense of humor was appreciated and much enjoyed.

DBS surgery also requires a patient to go off all Parkinson's meds 24 hours prior to the surgical procedure. The night before a very early morning pre-surgery appointment can be hellish. It was for David ... and somewhat for me. All his PD symptoms came back with a vengeance. We made it through, but it was grueling. The 4–5 hour surgery ended up being eight. Par for the Parkinson's course; a slow day with a wait that tarried.

Dave had signed an agreement allowing a resident to be in the operating room who was permitted to ask him questions at the end of surgery. The OR stay had been long for Dave, exceptionally long. And to this day, he remembers wanting to haul off and punch that student square in the nose, begging him to be done already. Dave was weary of being without his meds, not to mention being in a head lock from a halo during the operation *while he was awake*. It's incomprehensible, really. But it worked! DBS surgery was a huge success!

His medical team referred to Dave as the poster child of DBS. We watched his tremors settle down to a dead stop right before our eyes as the nurse practitioner used the remote to program the neuro-stimulator in his chest just a few days post-surgery. Those tremors came to a complete halt and never returned. He was able to cut his medication back by 2/3rds, which is helpful as the disease progresses. It felt a little bit like DBS had given David his life back, although it never promises to cure the disease. Only God can do that.

It was with great joy and gratitude that he recovered in the home of generous friends while I traveled back-and-forth between California and Pennsylvania. We had so much to be thankful for *and* that experience was hard. Really hard.

I flew across the country eight times and slept in seven different beds between mid-June and the end of August. I had to return home earlier than expected after receiving a frantic call from a concerned neighbor about our dog. That summer wore on me ... and on my resilience. However, there was no time to stop and recalibrate, I needed to get home to a very sick dog and leave my recovering husband in the care of friends and family. Discouragement barked at my heels as I left (no pun intended).

A Canine Crisis

Madden was a rescue. He was quirky, energetic, and affectionate, bringing Dave and me so much joy! But during that August, something went wrong. Terribly wrong. He had a hot spot on his stomach, and our neighbor noticed that it had broken the skin and was bleeding. I arranged for friends to come in and be with him around the clock during the day while our dogsitter worked, and until I could get back home. Madden digressed rapidly. This pup was a friend to anyone and everyone, but especially attentive and loyal to me. However, when I returned home, he would barely come near me. He slept curled up in the corner of the bathroom, whimpering and nearly breaking my heart. I literally did all I could to keep him alive until Dave was released to come home in early October. We had to put that sweet boy down days after Dave returned and we thought our hearts were going to break in two. It was hard.

During that troublesome stretch, our basement kept flooding while I was flying back and forth across the country. Once home or before leaving again, I would force myself to head down the basement steps (a few times at 4 in the morning before one of my kind and helpful girlfriends picked me up to go to the airport *again*) and each time I would pray out loud: Dear Jesus, please let there be no water on the floor. But it seemed every single time I stepped onto the basement linoleum, my feet splashed into an inch or more of water. Soon after that, it was discovered that the culprit was a sinkhole. You heard me right, a sinkhole! It was under the family room of our house, and then some. A gigantic cavity in the ground underneath where we lived. I know. We couldn't believe it either!

When Bobby Jenkins came to investigate our property, it ended with him telling us that ours was the largest residential sinkhole he had ever seen or repaired, and he had been in business for 35 years!!! It cost $36,000 to repair. It was hard. Really hard. And at that point, I was discouraged. Really, really discouraged.

"The story isn't over if the story isn't good."
— Cory Asbury, lyrics from the song, The Father's House

What came first, the chicken or egg? The disappointment or the trouble? Does it even matter? Discouragement and hopelessness are next in line, and you may have noticed that there's little to nothing beyond that. But hopelessness is never ever the end of the story for a Jesus follower. Hopelessness doesn't even have a seat at His table. I love that part of following Him: If the story isn't good, it's not over!

So, what changes the end of a story full of trouble and discouragement? Grace. Grace does. Grace changes our stories. And grace ushers in hope. I hope you'll hit pause long enough to go through your own stories and those of the ones you know and love. Stories that could have turned out so differently, tragic, hopeless. But didn't. That exercise gets me every single time I do it. Oh, there are some heartbreaking situations full of tragedy and heartache, but amazing grace comes in and changes us even if circumstances don't change. Hope changes the outcome *in us*. It's in the valleys where we become desperate for grace to show up in every ramification of our troubles and discouragement... and in his and in hers ... and in "this."

Maybe that's why we go to the valley; to become desperate for grace, for it's often in the Valley of Trouble where His grace collides with our discouragement. Face down in the valley is where we see all over again that Grace died for us while we were still flaunting our selfishness, missing God's mark, skipping out on His best (Romans 5:6, 8). It's where we become grateful for grace that goes beyond our human comprehension, requiring our spirit to grasp it and receive.

Grace was never meant to be achieved. Only received. So, right there on the ground floor of our deepest, darkest valley, Grace sits down next to us and begins declaring a different ending to our discouraging and troubled story while we try to catch our breath. And in that moment, we count on grace to be sufficient for the generations coming behind us.

Grace is Amazing

One of the most amazing things about grace is how it gently leads you and me to the gut-wrenching reality that my broken heart, my "dark side," my trouble isn't really all that different than yours. There is this astounding sense of camaraderie in amazing grace. Our trouble is much the same no matter how different it may look at first glance. Not always and not completely, but in the Valley of Trouble, we come to find out that we are fellow humans who are ultimately from the same family, the same seed, fallen in the same garden called Eden. A place where selfish longings trumped obedience to God and where lies were believed instead of refuted with truth. There I fall too. Over and over and over again.

And there in my valley I meet you, down on your luck and laying on the valley floor where, together, we notice that discouragement is one and the same for all, no matter what it is that troubles us. As a valley dweller who is following Jesus, we find that we're desperate for the same thing: God's amazing grace. And that sweet sound changes the end of the story, and so much more! Right there in that valley of heartache, grace shows up and saves a wretch like you … and like me.

Grace Can't Be Earned

When Grace saves us, it doesn't stop there, it truly is amazing that in the valley, or on the mountain top, grace invites you and me to note God's approval when we disapprove of ourselves and feel so unworthy. Trying to be worthy (or *get* worthy) makes grace no longer grace. I can't deserve it. You can't deserve it, and neither can he or she. We know that and, yet, when we're desperate for grace, religion can deceive us into thinking we can't have it unless we're worthy, so we try to earn it. And in believing that grace must be earned, we ashamedly withhold it from someone else because, after all, they just don't deserve it. And then it becomes a vicious cycle that turns our desperation for grace frantically needy, and there we discover that a sip from the fountain of grace is hardly enough.

A fire-hydrant of grace is more what we need. It's that reckless gush of grace that changes us, flooding our entire being with a God-perspective as it washes the limited earthly perspective down the drain. Drenched and dripping with grace, we can stand and begin to sway to a new melody within. The music that assists our dance with discouragement transposes into a melody assuring our hearts that there is still hope.

Biblical hope ... the kind of expectation that originates in suffering. Hope that doesn't "disappoint" as the Amplified version of Romans 5:5 explains, all because of the love of the Father.

His love, poured into His Son who has become our Savior, now pours into our veins and changes the pulse of everything. It transforms the movement on the dance floor. The rigid and calculated steps of our dance with disappointment becomes a free-spirited, twirling, and graceful flowing dance of hope. Hope in the what-ifs .... past, present and future ... hope for something beyond our discouraged selves. Hope for my broken heart and hope for yours with a united sigh of relief at the fountain of grace that becomes hope built on nothing less than Jesus' blood and righteousness. Hope in eternal salvation by way of grace.

> **Discouragement doesn't have to have the last word.**

It's a timeless melody heard only by those who come face-to-face with the Songwriter of grace in the valley of the shadow of death. The same Songwriter who became flesh and dwelt among us comes running into that Valley of Trouble to proclaim that the discouragement we feel today can become the hope we live tomorrow.

Hope invites us to ask a new what if question?

- What if it's true, and not just for me but also for you, not just in my valley but also in yours?
- What if the hope Jesus promised is free for the taking? (1 Peter 1:3-6).
- What if biblical hope is solid ground, not wishful thinking?
- What if that *is* the grace part of the Father letting you and me stumble into a Valley of Trouble to encounter Grace and hike out with a different mindset and renewed expectations?

Discouragement doesn't have to have the last word. A grace perspective is a glimpse of things as they *can* be one day, not as they are, and not as they feel today. Oh, thank God, not as they feel right now!

Our trouble may not go away. In fact, most of us have already learned the hard way that even when we come out of the valley, our trouble is good at following us and sticking around. Like really good at it! Trouble follows you and me around like a tired toddler whining nonstop, crying out, demanding, with empty pleas for more! Trouble becomes the house guest we never invited over. Sigh. Trouble has a way of outstaying it's welcome, but it's different with discouragement.

A discouraged heart isn't allowed to stay unless we keep the door open. Discouragement may have moved in, but she has to leave when we say so, making it clear that she's not welcome back any time soon! We may not be able to make Trouble leave, but we certainly have every right to demand that Discouragement pack her bags and go for good! We must speak directly to our hearts as the Psalmist did with poignant questions and a wise command: *"Why are you so downcast my soul? Why are you so disturbed within me? Put. Your. Hope. In. God." (Psalm 42:5).*

A Reversal of Roles

Do you ever talk to God like he's sitting in the passenger's seat and headed to the grocery store with you? I do, and often. It may seem odd to some, but recently God and I were engaged in conversation, if you could call it that when one person is doing all the talking. Smile. He's a masterful listener and it was no different that afternoon when I decided to remind Him all about the quintessential damsel in distress I tend to be, and if He hadn't noticed for 26 of our 37 years of marriage, Dave took good care of me. Like, really good care.

You know by now that Dave and I are wired differently. He's great at all things financial, following instruction manuals, fixing things inside and out of the house, keeping our cars clean, and more. He's athletic, brilliant in a crisis, understated and humble in his approach to all things. On the other hand, I have an aversion to doing things I'm not very good at, especially when my husband is. Dave took such good care of me and of our family while the kids were growing up, that being required to take care of myself has been nothing short of staggering. But for now, let's return to the dialogue in the car which was more like a monologue.

I blabbed on and on to God about how much I don't like being the one who oversees all things Jameson, not because I'm lazy (well, maybe a little), but because I'm not good at it. And because it quickly morphs from task to burden. I tend to talk *at* God about things as if He doesn't already know. It's laughable, really. But I intentionally try not to grumble and complain to Him, nor to Dave. Lately I have failed miserably at both, and I'm confident both of them would concur.

Being needed nearly 24/7 after living an entire lifetime seeking and putting high value on independence is hard, and in moments, discouraging. Very discouraging. This reversal of roles in our marriage is not something I could've ever imagined and certainly would never have chosen. That's how trouble is and, quite frankly, that's why it's so discouraging. Trouble forces life to act differently than we could ever have imagined. It doesn't ask for permission to show up and never considers one's level of comfort. Trouble is a rude intruder.

Dave and I dreamed and planned and banked on retirement in San Diego. Those dreams were easy to imagine, as we had been living them out temporarily for decades while on vacation there year after year visiting my extended family. Fast forward to now: we are actually residents in North County, San Diego. Since we arrived, not one plan or dream has transpired into real life. Well, other than living here and living close to one of our sons and his family and enjoying life with our first grandchild. And for that we are deeply grateful. It should be enough, but instead, I find myself often more discouraged than I want to be. You understand; you, too, have plans and dreams that were hijacked by troubles in your life.

Restrictions of Parkinson's Disease

Dave's Parkinson's and chronic leg pain restricts him from walking on his own, driving, boxing, enjoying his independence. Parkinson's demanded he sell Big Bertha (the name I gave his beloved Harley) before leaving Arizona, and any work he does requires regular intervals of rest. He can only hold our precious granddaughter while sitting. Mornings and stairs are no longer his friends, and the delight of going to church has turned into a chore. He longs to serve others, feed and bless the homeless, help me, our family and others, but instead he needs me, our family, and others *to help him*.

To say that the life we live is vastly different than the dreams and plans of our conversations over 37 years of marriage would be a gross understatement. Anybody else? Every one of us walks through days that hold some measure of disappointment about what we can't or want to do, and many of them leave us fighting off discouragement like a pesky fly. We swing and swat but miss the annoying little pest over and over again. We stare at the wall as if in a trance in hopes of trapping the fly between the swatter and drywall in an effort to squash him once and for all. But that imaginary fly swatter seems to more often stay clean while discouragement buzzes around our house, frustrating us and breaking down our resolve to master it.

Take Heart

You do know there's a power behind what's troubling you, right? The power of darkness, the enemy of your soul; Satan is to blame. He's the accuser who thrives on finding ways to kill our joy, steal our peace, and destroy our faith and relationships, including the one we have (or want to have) with God. Satan is the power that tries to hold over us the temptation to give up, just like he tempted Jesus both in the wilderness and on the cross. But Jesus subdued the influence of darkness that tries to beat us up with doubt, discouragement, and offense in our seasons of suffering.

Biblical hope can instruct our souls in meaningful ways, giving us reason to rest long enough to catch our breath. And while we rest, we can grab an imaginary highlighter and mark the last half of what Jesus said in John 16:33 on the pages of our souls, and maybe even literally on the pages of our Bibles: *"I have overcome the world."* It's the only relief I've found for the overwhelming weariness of trouble that tempts me to give in to discouragement, to give up and quit. Jesus was clear in stating that in the world you and I will be well-acquainted with trouble, and then he added:

> *"But take heart! I have overcome the world!"*
> *John 16:33b NIV*

Jesus. Has. Overcome. We believe that. At least in theory. But we want to believe with all our might that because he has, we, too, can overcome the assignment that trouble has delivered.

To overcome in Greek means "to subdue."[36] That's it! You and I want to subdue and quiet the rage of trouble before it shows up at the front door with discouragement on its arm. This declaration of Jesus is a game changer for you and me: He overcame so we can overcome! Jesus did exactly what we long to do — He overcame the world we live in! A world full of trouble. He still overcomes. He subdues the world. My world and your world. His overcoming power is in us, and His overcoming power is for us.

We can confidently rest in His promises and catch our breath even while the troubles of our lives swirl around us. There's always hope wherever the words of Jesus are welcomed. And hope puts discouragement on pause or, better yet, hope hits delete and discouragement is done for! There really is a way to get through without giving up, and it's just on the other side of catching our breath.

> **There's always hope wherever the words of Jesus are welcomed.**

A List of Troubles

In many ways, you could say that my whole life has been strung together by a long list of troubles I've encountered throughout the decades. Yours probably has too. In fact, most people could list their troubles and make mine pale in comparison. But this book isn't about comparing misery. It's about something we all share in common; this journey on earth holds trouble. Lots of it for most of us. The enemy works overtime to convince us that we're "the only one" this or that has ever happened to. But he's a liar. This journey on earth holds trouble for every single one of us. We're in it together. And whatever the trouble might be, it escorts discouragement right up and into our hearts and homes.

I had a personal laundry list of difficulties that shoved me into the Valley of Trouble marked by heartache, difficulty, and trials. It was lengthy, although I didn't know that. Not until the Holy Spirit inspired me to take inventory and chronicle the things I had endured. It was staggering to see them in black and white; the troubles of my life stacked up in one big handwritten pile.

Jesus was right about expected tribulation, that's the sad truth. But Jesus never ever leaves us hanging with bad news alone. He's a truth-teller. After all, *He is the truth* (John 1:14; John 14:6). He's also a hope-giver, and the statement He made on the heels of the promise that in the world we will have affliction is saturated with hopeful expectation: Jesus has overcome the world! Past tense. In other words, Jesus *overcame*! He took the very power of the enemy head on, and He prevailed! Trouble has been subdued by the power of the Living God! Jesus has overcome the world! We don't have to be a victim to the enemy's control who tries to insist that Trouble can boss us around.

We don't have to listen to the narrative that tells us we should just give up because Trouble just won't leave us alone. We can preach to ourselves and say a fanatic "no" to the power of suffering. We *can* get through whatever we're facing. The enemy is defeated, we don't have to be! When we trust Jesus, we, too, can subdue the power of darkness as Jesus gives our pain purpose, heals what's broken, takes ashes and, making something beautiful out of them, turns grief and sadness into joyful dancing. He's a master at taking bad things and squeezing good out of them. He's overcome the world, and in Him, we can too! That's what He came to earth to do, even though he warned us about the troubles of life (John 10:10).

Getting Unstuck

Since we are in Christ and He lives in us, why do we sometimes find ourselves stuck in the quicksand of discouragement instead of on the mountain top overcoming? (1 Corinthians 1:30-31, Galatians 2:20). I've been puzzled by that myself at times, frustrated, feeling like a failure.

For more years than I care to count, my feet were sinking in the sand of discouragement. Try as I may, I just could not climb out but, instead, battled a feeling of despair as I stood in the mushy mixture of sand and water unable to overcome. Even though Jesus had. Discouragement painted my days until the Holy Spirit drew me to the quiet with pen and paper. He told me it was time to make a list. A laundry list of the significant troubles and heartaches I had endured throughout my life, those people and things I had lost.

Laboriously, I obeyed. Genuinely, I tasted release. Staring down the layers of losses I had experienced was restorative. It began to set me free from chronic discouragement as the Healer pulled my feet, and my heart, from the sinking sand.

It was with each list item that I grieved again, some for the very first time. My lament over some losses was mild, and other loss was deeply sorrowful. I discovered that I had been unable to move past the pain of no longer having who or what I once did, or what I should have had but never did. I had to see the pain that loss created in me. Acknowledge the pain. Own the pain.

So, for the discouraged and dismayed, sometime in your schedule soon:

- hit pause
- grab pen and paper
- make your own list
- read over it
- sit with it
- grieve and own the pain of each loss
- see if you don't feel the quicksand loosening around your feet and discouragement loosening from the death grip it's had on your soul

Writing and grieving your list can place your feet on solid ground again, and discouragement will begin to feel like an old friend who just doesn't visit any more. Once you laboriously obey, whether on your own or in the presence of a trusted friend or counselor, note that it's easier to catch your breath when you face reality instead of turning away and wishing life were different. Be honest about your feelings as you surrender and accept what is and begin to breathe again. The Holy Helper will sit down beside you and give you a new language; it's the language and reality of overcoming.

BREATHE DEEPLY

"Breathing is the first thing we do when we are born,
and the last thing we do before we die, yet most of us
pay little attention to it throughout our lives."
– Author Unknown

INHALE

Isaiah 61:1-4
Lamentations 3:18-24
Romans 5:1-5
2 Corinthians 4:7-11

EXHALE

- Choose a verse, a sentence or just a phrase from one of the passages above.[37]
- Write it down on something you can post in your home, office or car, or at least carry with you.
- Meditate on its meaning; think about it again and again (and again!) over the course of your day/week.
- Read it in context.
- Read it in other Bible versions; the Amplified and Passion Translation are favorites.
- Look up the meaning of the words that you want to better understand.
- Memorize the verse or passage.
- Let the verse or phrase run around on the inside of you until it becomes your very own, part of your DNA.
- Consider personalizing it by inserting your name, or praying it for yourself, someone else, or for a situation.

seven
UNSETTLED

*"I would have despaired had I not believed that I would see
the Lord's goodness in the land of living!
Wait for and confidently expect the Lord;
Be strong and let your heart take courage ..."*

Psalm 27:13-14a AMP

don't tend to get attached to things. I get attached to people. Very attached. I'm not particularly sentimental and I love to purge, so packing up a house of 24 years of living when we left Pennsylvania to move west was, for the most part, enjoyable for me.

That is until it came time for the new owners to pick up the oversized red floral couch that held so much of my heart, family time, and was saturated with things the Lord had done for my family, close friends, the daughters, my heart, and friends who felt like family. That couch held stories and community, tears and prayers, laughter and together time, revelation from the Lord for me and those I sat with there. It was drenched with memories from 24 years of living and, as it left our home, my heart began to flip and flop within, and an overwhelming sense of being unsettled began to grow. It hit me; we were leaving State College for good, the place our boys knew as home and the place I made home. We were leaving and we wouldn't be returning anytime soon. State College, a place I didn't want to call home and now it was the only place that felt like home.

I stood alone in our empty and much-loved house that would soon no longer be ours and listened to my own sobs echo off the empty walls and packed boxes surrounding me. I felt as though I had been pushed into a corner where, momentarily, I began to wonder how the Lord's goodness could show up for me there in that house that was no longer mine, and our new house on the southwest side of the country was yet to be built. Unsettled. Not a pleasant place to be. I know I'm stating the obvious, but seriously.

Being unsettled is evoked by the unfamiliar, magnified by a lack of connection, and perpetuated by transition. Unsettled means that things are not yet resolved, things that matter. That's the hard part. It's one thing to feel unsettled living in a new city not knowing your way around, but being unsettled about something like moving to an unfamiliar place, navigating a difficult relationship, receiving a terrifying medical diagnosis, desperately longing for a baby or a significant other, not having enough money to cover the essentials, dealing with tension at work or conflict at home, being concerned for a wayward or struggling child, being overlooked, betrayed, or any other disruptive or troubling situation, can be absolutely unnerving. That kind of unsettling will most often throw us off balance and shove us into a corner where we feel on edge and anxious, wondering if the Lord's goodness can show up for us, for "this."

Unsettled is a state of being we really like to avoid. We want things to be settled and when they're not, we want to know how to fix them, understand why they're happening, and know when they might be, well, settled again. Feeling unsettled has a dashboard of panic buttons we are tempted to push to convince ourselves we are *not* going to come undone. That's the threat; this thing that has me unsettled might make me unravel. And that is not something we want to happen.

When Unsettled Meets Courage

Picture sitting on my red floral couch in your imagination, having a conversation about the five daughters of Zelophehad (try saying that name quickly 10 times). Do you know their short story recorded in the Old Testament book of Numbers? I didn't either until I ran across a verse with a list of their names that grabbed my attention and made me curious. It's a remarkable account. These sisters found themselves desperately unsettled and used it as a chance to bravely seek change.

The book of Numbers chronicles the 40-year journey of the Israelites led by Moses from Mount Sinai to the very edge of Canaan, the Promised Land. Numbers 26:33 is where Zelophehad's daughters are introduced, and we know little else about them beyond what's recorded in their short story in chapter 27.[38]

They had reason to feel unsettled, which may be an understatement on my part. Their father had died in the wilderness just before entering the Promised Land; there is no mention of their mother. The death of a father for unmarried daughters in their culture, no matter their age (which I could not find), would have been very disturbing, maybe even terrifying, as they found themselves orphaned and traditionally having no legal right to their inheritance. That would have been buried with their dad.

Yet it is in the brief account we learn that these brave sisters request a meeting with Moses to ask for the family inheritance, an inconceivable thing for daughters to do! In fact, it would have been unheard of for an Israelite woman to go before male leadership to request anything, let alone five of them to go together. And on top of that, they were questioning the law of inheritance. Such. A. Thing. Just. Did. Not. Happen. And yet it did.

So, in a few verses in Numbers, we read about their earnest plea to Moses that begins by honoring their dad. They remind Moses, and the others, that their late father had not been numbered among the ones who rebelled as recorded in Numbers chapter 26. But the punch line of the girl's request was to ask for their father's allotted land. This appeal doesn't strike us as audacious nor necessarily frightening because, after all, the girls should be entitled to their family inheritance, right? Wrong.

This was a big deal. A very big deal that must have taken an exorbitant amount of courage, and I don't think it would be a stretch to say it took more faith than a grain of mustard seed for them to believe they had a bright future in Canaan apart from their dad. According to the law and custom of Israel, being given the family inheritance would seem like a lost cause, given the circumstances, because wives and daughters had no inheritance apart from a husband or father. Talk about feeling unsettled! And let's note that at this point in time, Israel had not possessed even an inch of land in Canaan, yet these sisters came asking for their father's rightful allotment among their relatives, believing they would enter and live on the land like all the others.

Interestingly, maybe more like amazingly, Moses listened to the girls and took their request before the Lord, which is the first moment of seeming victory for the girls. But I have to wonder if Moses was flabbergasted by their supplication. He surely had not been confronted with this before, and particularly not by females. Scripture isn't clear about that, but I often try to imagine what might have happened between the verses and chapters in biblical accounts.

Regardless, with wisdom, Moses seeks the Lord, and we discover that he was not the only one who entertained the daughter's request; the Lord heard their plea long before Moses had. God told Moses that the girls were right in asking and further instructs him to change the law of inheritance. So, based on the five sisters' brave inquiry, Moses establishes a new statute in Israel; when a father dies and has no son, his inheritance will be transferred to his daughter. Holy wow! Out of this unnerving space of uncertainty came courage that ultimately established a new-ordinance-become-law by the daughters of Zelophehad!

Pause a moment and let the magnitude of that sink into your spirit and know that, out of your season of being desperately unsettled, courageous acts by faith can rise up in you too! Choices, decisions, acts born of faith will always hold the potential of opening a door of possibility for others, sometimes for many generations to come. There was so much more to the sister's story than being orphaned, shoved in a corner of life wondering how, when, where, what. The "more" was ultimately dependent on their refusal to give in to the circumstances they were given and a determination to make an unprecedented choice to do the hard thing. The sisters trusted that the God of their late father still had good on His heart for them and bravely used their faith to recall His goodness and looked up to see Him show up.

Recalling God's Goodness and Character

Could it be that Zelophehad's faith shaped that of his five daughters, and his noble character influenced their boldness? I have a hunch it did. Regardless, in their grief and surely in a head space of being totally unsettled, I think their late daddy would have been so proud of his brave, faith-filled daughters.

In fact, I wonder if these sisters knew about their father's inheritance and believed the land rightfully belonged to them *because* their dad often talked about it? Could it be that he taught them to dream about life in Canaan and their future there as a family? They seem to have a clear picture of a bright and hopeful future for themselves in the Promised Land, a very uncommon response for orphaned women. Did their dad help them believe they were or could be strong, capable women whose voice had value?

It seems to me that their courage and faith may have been bolstered by someone. Their response was unusual and ultimately, it changed the course of history, the basis for a new law of inheritance. It's remarkable really. And just like with Zelophehad's daughters, courage and faith can be birthed in you and me during a season of feeling, or literally being, unsettled. Could the memory of their earthly father's goodness have given birth to their seemingly fresh measure of faith and renewed confidence even in their grief-induced unsettling circumstances?

The story of these five young women reminds you and me that, even in an unsettling situation, hope can arise! It's the infamous truth in Isaiah 40 in real time: As we wait on Jehovah, our inner strength is fortified and we can soar to new heights of understanding, able to trust God and act courageously instead of getting stuck in what's unsettling us, shrinking in fear or giving up (Isaiah 40:31).

God goes before you and me to make a way through what we're facing as we recall His goodness and past faithfulness, renewing our trust in His character, and bravely doing what we must. That's the kind of faith and courage that are often born during a season of being unsettled, uneasy, or anxious about the future whether that future is tomorrow or next year.

The key to waiting on the Lord as He strengthens us from the inside out is to make time to remember His goodness. Recalling God's goodness is what settles and recalibrates our hearts, not the situations of our lives resolved. It's in seeing His goodness in the land we find ourselves living where new measures of faith and courage can be regained. The more unsettled we allow ourselves to become, the more difficult it is to trust the sovereignty of God, or our ability to do what we must about that which is seeking to unravel us.

Glory from the Red Floral Couch

Recalling the good heart of the Father was often the glory of my red floral couch. His good intentions were discovered for the first time, or all over again, ushering in trust and confidence in His way and that strengthened and balanced unsettled hearts. Those who sat there left differently than when they had arrived, often walking away more steady and more hopeful about their own good future than when they sat down, including me. We all need a place we go when the winds of feeling unsettled begin to swirl around us. A place where we can intentionally recall the goodness of God even in the harshness of life. A place set aside to open our Bibles, look up to heaven, and catch our breath as we remember God's faithfulness in days gone by.

> **Recalling God's goodness is what settles and recalibrates our hearts, not the situations of our lives resolved.**

It's there that we remind ourselves that acts of courage by faith are not taken lightly in the kingdom of heaven (Hebrews 11:6). Faith and courage change our own perspective and can make a difference for others as well. Who can know what brave response will be stirred in the heart of someone else because of the influence of our faith? Jesus told his disciples that faith can move mountains, cause trees to be cast into the sea, make the impossible, possible.

Faith reminds us to look up. It strengthens our hearts and deposits hope in the hearts and lives of others! No matter your gender or what has unraveled in your life, you, too, can have a heart like the daughters of Zelophehad and that bravely fight for your inheritance in Christ, and so much more! May we ever be aware that, although we may not notice someone watching us navigate unsettling circumstances, they are! Many can be influenced by our courageous and faith-filled choices in ways we simply cannot fathom and may not know until we get to heaven.

Never ever underestimate the power of your courage by faith in large or small acts of obedience. Every single one matters and has the potential to change your heart, and that of someone else, and maybe even the course of history. We are on this journey called life together, and as Jesus followers, we need each other.

The Impetus to Look Up

Courage and faith, born in a season of being unsettled, can be the impetus to lift our heads from the distraction of whatever feels unsettling, and *look up!* Research reveals that pedestrian related accidents caused by texting and walking have increased, and now outnumber accidents by texting and driving, which is something I find rather startling, and probably need to take a lesson from before becoming a casualty myself.[39]

But that's not the most imminent danger of having our heads down, although it is of great importance. It's more about missing the moment right in front of us or, far more sadly, the person right in front of us. Imagine how differently the story could have ended if Zelophehad's daughters had kept their heads down in grief, worry, and fear. How might it have looked on the long haul if they had let their dad's death not only cause them to feel unsettled, but actually unravel them from the inside out? Those sisters had to look up in order to be brave enough to make a plea for their inheritance and good future in Canaan.

What do you and I miss when we don't look up? It could be far more significant than we could even imagine.

Living on Autopilot

A young mom and her five-ish year-old daughter came into the nail salon where I was getting a pedicure. My chair sat right next to the cheerful little girl, and with my own joy, I watched them choose their nail polish. After cleaning her tiny feet, the nail tech began to paint bright pink polish on the child's ever so tiny toenails. She was giddy and wanted her mommy to see her new toes. I'm sure her mother really did want to see them but, instead, seemed consumed with her own cell phone. Soon I began to think I might have to pull my feet off the pedestal and leave with an unfinished pedicure because it became unsettling to watch this precious little daughter incessantly tapping on her mommy's arm saying over and over, "Mommy, look at my toes! Mommy, look at my toes! Mooooommmmy! MOM!MEEEE! Pleeease look at my toes!" Finally, the mother looked up for a split second and said something to the effect of, "Oh, how pretty!" but in a nano second, she was back to phone gazing.

As I lifted my pointer finger in my head, and in judgment of the darling young mom, I couldn't help but notice three pointing back me. I suspect that mama may look up from her life one day to notice a budding and beautiful teenage girl in front of her who she hardly recognizes and wonder where the years have gone. But let's bring that thought home, what might we look up from one day to notice we have missed with our heads down and our hearts distracted? It would behoove all of us, whether we're in a parenting season or not, whether we're unsettled or not, to ask ourselves, "What am I missing when my head, my gaze, my attention is downward?"

Living on autopilot, allowing our minds and lives to always be busy, full, overscheduled, can be an illusion of our importance. It can also keep us from noticing the person, or the miracle, planted right in front of us, or the new thing God is longing to do (2 Corinthians 5:17). When we live with our heads down and become increasingly more enamored with someone else's reality (think social media), connected to our past or worried about our future, it can hold us hostage, yearning for a different moment and experience than the one we're in.

Looking up from our devices, or the vain imaginations in our heads, can begin to release us from feeling unsettled. Our addiction, or at best, our infatuation, with being connected *all the time* can keep us in an unsettled state of being. Too often we can be found looking down, missing the moment right smack in front of us.

> **Our addiction, or at best, our infatuation, with being connected all the time can keep us in an unsettled state of being.**

God is in the moments of your life and mine (Ephesians 5:15-16 TPT). He's standing in our good future inviting us to press toward Him and the good things He has for us. It would be wise, therefore, to do an about-face into the future with our heads up, fully engaged.

Looking up is a heart-wide-open posture … a dependent posture … a surrendered posture … a faith posture. Looking up is a posture that can settle a chaotic heart, and dare I say, a chaotic life, faster than you or I can scroll through social media posts. Look up, friends, the Spirit of the Living God is in the moments. Let's not miss even one of them, for when we live in His goodness and steadfast love, a gift each and every morning on earth, it can settle our hearts (Lamentations 3:22-23).

As Jesus followers, let's be known as a people who habitually look up and pay attention to what God is trying to show us. He seeks to partner with us in carrying out His plans for our lives and the lives of those around us (John 15:4-5). And when we look up, we just might see or hear exactly what we need to soothe our unsettled souls, like the sound from heaven declaring "I love you!" over us again and again!

The Banner of Our Allegiance

"He brought me to the banqueting table,
and His banner over me is love."
Song of Soloman 2:4

The context of the book of Song of Soloman is actually a romance between two lovers meant to be an allegory of God's longing to be in a love relationship with His people, His beloved bride. I once heard a preacher describe God's banner over us as the "I Love You Banner." Amen to that! So, when we are unsettled, if we will look up and be reminded of God's goodness that is being declared in the heavenly realm as His never ending "I love you" to each one of us, it can be a game-changer.

The Father's "I love you" became reality through the death, burial, and resurrection of His only Son, Jesus (John 3:16-17), and when we take time to meditate on that reality alone, it can settle our hearts. Think about a banner in the natural realm that you might see waving during a tailgate at a football game; banners declare whose team someone is rooting for. Banners wave in the sky to make a statement about one's allegiance. God's banner, His allegiance, is about His sacrificial love for you and for me.

When you and I start to feel unsettled, we can look up and see His "I Love You" waving above us in the heavenly realm.

- When you feel unsettled and fear is relentless, look up; His banner over you is love.
- When disappointment nags at your heart, look up; His banner over you is love.
- When you find yourself standing at an unfamiliar crossroad wondering where, when, how, what's next, look up; His banner over you is love.
- When you need to get from here-to-there and indecision threatens, look up; His banner over you is love.
- When there seems to be no good way out, look up. Choose the opposite of dread. Look up with hopeful expectation; His banner over you is love.
- Look up. The Father in heaven is forever seeking ways to reveal Himself to you in greater measure.
  - the magnitude of His love
  - the loyalty of His love
  - the attentiveness of His love
  - the tenacity of His love
  - the splendor of His love
  - the tenderness of His love
  - the security in His love

  Look up!
- When life is hard and pounds your heart with worry, look up; His banner over you is His declaration of loyal love that will never turn its back on you.

- When the next step seems insurmountable and fills your heart with overwhelming concern, look up; His banner over you is His declaration of fierce love that fights for you, day and night.

- When the future is uncertain and dread begins to dictate, look up; His banner over you is His assurance that you are the apple of His eye and nothing and no one can touch you without His permission.

- When you feel alone and overlooked, as if nobody cares, look up; His banner over you is an invitation to come to the banqueting house as His beloved son or daughter. His love will always shun your fear. It is not welcome in His house. It will be turned away every time it tries to enter. So, look up and join Him there.

- When your heart is unsettled, look up; His banner over you is love, a love that, when received, will strengthen your legs and your resolve, making you sturdy and able to press on.

His banner over you, and the one over me, is a statement of His allegiance to keep on loving us. And when we forget, we can simply look up and be reminded that, all day long, our God declares His devotion by the gifts of life He's given, and by the truth of His Word that both shout: "I love you, child! I love you! I love you! I love you!"

As you let that reality run around on the inside of your being, you'll find that you can catch your breath once again while His goodness and love settle your heart before the next sunrise. That's a promise you and I can count on!

> *"The splendor-light of heaven's glorious sunrise is*
> *about to break upon us in holy visitation, all because*
> *the merciful heart of our God is so very tender."*
> *Zechariah's Prophecy of Jesus in Luke 1:78 TPT*

BREATHE DEEPLY

"When you stop and take several deep breaths: a long inhalation through the nose and a long exhalation through the mouth, you turn on the 'rest & digest' function, which is the exact opposite of fight, flight or freeze. You can literally reset your system in those moments."
- JoAnn Foley-DeFiore, PhD.
Teaching Professor of Biobehavioral Health

INHALE

Numbers 27:1-11
Psalm 34
Psalm 121
Psalm 123

EXHALE

- Choose a verse, a sentence or just a phrase from one of the passages above.[40]
- Write it down on something you can post in your home, office or car, or at least carry with you.
- Meditate on its meaning; think about it again and again (and again!) over the course of your day/week.
- Read it in context.
- Read it in other Bible versions; the Amplified and Passion Translation are favorites.
- Look up the meaning of the words that you want to better understand.
- Memorize the verse or passage.
- Let the verse or phrase run around on the inside of you until it becomes your very own, part of your DNA.
- Consider personalizing it by inserting your name, or praying it for yourself, someone else, or for a situation.

eight
UNFAIR

"When you go through a trial, the sovereignty of God
is the pillow upon which you lay your head."

- CHARLES SPURGEON[41]

My husband and I raised two sons who couldn't possibly be wired more differently in personality and perspective. If you have children, you know exactly what I'm talking about, and it's likely that you know, even if you don't.

Our firstborn tends to see the world in black-and-white with an intrinsic bent towards justice in the world. His brother is more open-ended with an intrinsic bent toward understanding the world. Andy, our youngest, would often wisely say, "everything happens for a reason" to which Ben, our oldest, would often walk away with a frustrated chip on his shoulder that implied he wanted to *know* the reason.

I don't remember Ben's exact age nor the exact context of the conversation that led to a common topic of discussion, the injustice of any given situation. I do, however, recall with clarity, Ben's vehement response to my prompting him once again to keep in mind that "life isn't fair." His young mind had heard me say that a few too many times, and he blurted back with a vengeance, "BUT I WANT IT TO BE FAIR!"

Ooof, I hear ya, kid. So does your mama. I hate the reality that it's not and never will be. In fact, nothing I've ever tried has made it so. But don't get me wrong, I desperately want it to be fair too. Jesus warned us it would not ever be. Not on this earth anyway.

I personally want life to be fair … and good … and easy … without pain, and hassle free. You probably do too. As a mom, I contemplated early on that to be a "good" mom, my intention should be about finding ways to prepare our children for a life that I knew all too well would surely hold disappointments, setbacks, losses, failures, and far too much heartache and injustice. Mine had. Instead, however, my mother's heart preferred to *shield* Ben and Andy from impending and promised trouble.

But Jesus is the One who promised it; there will be trouble in this world that we call home. It would behoove me to take note. Our children, and others we love, discover that reality whether we try to shield them from it or not. And the One who promised it, endured it. We must too. We can't escape trouble in life, the injustice and the heartache on this earthly journey, although we certainly give it our best shot.

Jesus surrendered to it, knowing the injustice of earth couldn't begin to compare to the joy of heaven. He endured the cross, knowing ahead of time there would be great joy as each one of us was adopted into God's family through salvation. He kept His heart and mind fixed on that coming good, and off the injustice He was experiencing.

Life isn't fair and that's terribly disappointing. In fact, in moments it's infuriating, but Jesus rewrites the script and sets joy before us so that we, too, can endure. The apostle Peter reminds us that Jesus was our example in suffering; He didn't sin nor retaliate but instead, entrusted Himself to the One who judges all things rightly (1 Peter 2:21-24). The Father in heaven will bring justice in His way to all that is unjust in ours.

High Hopes Dashed

I apprehensively scrolled through my contacts even though it was barely the cusp of a new day at the beginning of a new week. I felt desperate for an alternative way to get Dave downstairs to the first-floor carport of our beach rental as we headed to the Emergency Room. I held high hopes that we could get him into the mostly unused and very temperamental elevator on the property where our beach rental was housed on the middle floor of the 3-story building.

It had been about 24 hours since Dave was able to bear weight or walk on his left foot. We would soon come to find out that he was having a flareup of pseudogout in his ankle. Yep, you read that right, pseudogout. I know, we had never heard of such a thing before either. How unfair to have pseudogout when you already have PD! We would soon learn that an unexpected diagnosis does not prevent anyone from enduring another unusual one, or more. Injustice never takes into account what difficulties or discriminations are already on the resume of its victim.

> **Injustice never takes into account what difficulties or discriminations are already on the resume of its victim.**

It was good they found a reason for Dave's pain, but during the hours of not knowing what was wrong, the panic (and the pain) was real and felt unfair. After-all, he was already trying to enjoy vacation with PD limitations and now something unrelated. Pseudogout; pseudo meaning the pain manifests as gout due to calcium build up in a joint that crystallizes causing unmanageable, gout-like pain. That is a laymen's description paraphrased by me from the ER doc. So, on top of Dave's typical "postural instability," aka balance issues due to Parkinson's Disease, he couldn't walk without assistance.

Trust me when I say that the combination of PD and pseudogout made hopping on one leg down the cement stairs outside our unit out of the question, although he argued otherwise. He was only able to move from one place to another slowly, and painstakingly, when both of his hands were firmly gripping both of my shoulders. If only you could have seen us in the middle of the night when mother nature called. Funny. Not funny. Sorry for the visual.

This would be our second trip to Scripps Memorial Emergency Room during our annual beach vacation because, you know everybody loves to spend their vacation days at the ER, right? Smile. But our repeated trek proved productive this time as the ER doctor on duty got to the root of the issue and prescribed the right medication like a champ. We were grateful, and relieved! In fact, although still hobbling, Dave got progressively better over the next 24 hours. Much better in fact. But again, who knew there was such a thing as pseudogout? Who knew that such a condition could press one's heart like it did mine? The weight was so heavy while the voice of fear barked orders at me and demanded my attention over every other voice in my head.

Fear is like that. It shows up unannounced and often unnoticed, at least at first. It wastes no time before it begins to hiss and whisper every possible worst-case scenario. It gets louder and louder as it lies to one's soul, and then lies again. It never plays fair, and anything that causes panic, dread, and keeps its victim on edge will do. It's no different on vacation. Fear threatened: This is the beginning of the end ... Dave may never walk again ... life as you've known it is about to change ... PD is taking the upper hand ... and on and on the voice of fear clamored. It badgered me with questions: How are you going to get him home? How are the two of you going to live alone if Dave can't walk? What if he must be hospitalized? Or worse yet, what if this is Parkinson's related and he can't live at home at all?

The questions that fear relentlessly inquired of me made my heart pound harder and harder as they yapped like a dog startled by the doorbell and began to drain faith from my soul. Fast forward to later that same day, past the second ER visit, when I began to feel the weight of what I needed to do; muster up the energy to talk back to fear even though Dave was on the mend. The late afternoon soon turned into evening and then bedtime. As I reached up to twist off the small switch hidden in the lampshade on our nightstand, I promised myself to rise before dawn to watch the earth's morning ritual. I knew it was time to tune my heart to hear the Voice that calls the shots in my life, and worship Him alone in the quiet of the morning sunrise.

Slipping out of bed just before the alarm at 5:57, I quietly crept down the cold tile hallway and through the kitchen to flip the on-switch of the Hamilton Beach coffee maker before heading to the deck that overlooked the bay. Once outside, I turned over the dew-drenched cushions to the dry side and stacked my Bible, journal, and a book onto the knee-high plastic patio table before going back inside for my cuppa joe. I prepared to gaze at the beauty of the sunrise and worship the Creator of the dawn as I carefully lowered myself onto the seat cushion while steadying my full mug, and gently scootched back into the Adirondack chair before resting my head back.

> **Worship turns our hearts from being fixated on the injustice right in front of us to gaze upon the goodness and mercy of heaven above us.**

After taking a few deep breaths, I began to talk to myself. Life was once again feeling unfair as trouble and heartache piled up. Couldn't we cut a break for one short week of vacation? But I know well that our words matter when life is treating us unfairly. Words carry power, even the ones to ourselves. Especially the ones to ourselves. As I talked to me and entered sunrise worship, I began to talk to Him.

Worship turns our hearts from being fixated on the injustice right in front of us to gaze upon the goodness and mercy of heaven above us.

I spoke to my internal world, telling myself to anchor again to the King of my heart.

- Worship redirects a fearful heart.
- Worship runs to Jesus, and, just like Jairus in the New Testament, expects Him to show up and command life to overcome the death that's currently knocking on our door.
- Worship reminds our hearts that God is bigger than what we're facing, sovereign over our questions, and ever running to our rescue when all else is threatening to take us down.
- Worship changes us even when our situation stays exactly the same.
- Worship doesn't need the sunrise nor the morning, but it does need a surrendered heart that will let go of its burden to become mindful of His worth.

Worship redirects our eyes from the trance-like stare on what's unfair to the beauty of the Man of Sorrows familiar with suffering and grief because suffering is always attached to injustice in some way (Isaiah 53:3).

It's in the unfairness of our suffering where we tend to beg God to do something drastic. By nature, we want justice and at least some kind of "sweet" revenge. Christy Johnston, author of *Releasing Prophetic Solutions*, unpacks a kingdom response to what is unjust that transcends our human longing for God's judgment when life proves unfair. She explains that abiding in the presence of the Lord is the foundation on which supernatural solutions are inspired, "His kingdom is both love and justice, but under the reign of the New Covenant, the cross and the resurrection, the covenant of grace, mercy, and redemption, Jesus becomes the kiss of mercy to a dying and hurting world …. Rather than praying over the problem and begging God for a solution or calling down his judgment, we get to boldly come before him, and *have him share the secret solutions that are stored up in heaven for the problems around us.*"[42] (Italics are mine)

God has solutions in heaven for problems on earth, and as His children, we are invited to confidently approach His throne to find mercy and grace for what we need. This truth is such a glorious summons from heaven for the injustice we endure on earth. There are no guarantees that injustice will be rectified, at least not down here. The only thing we can bank on is the One who judges righteously can be trusted.

So, back to that summer morning, let's pick up when I needed sunglasses as I turned the thin pages of my hard copy Passion Translation Bible to the gospel of Luke, chapter eight. Once again, I was making my way through the gospels, as I typically do at the start of each new year. However, on this particular year, that devotional journey was hijacked by the untimely death of my very dear friend who was like a sister. I sat on the second story deck taking in the reflection of morning on the water while gazing at the August sunrise peering over the condos on the east side of the bay.

I reflected on memories created with Jess and our husbands right there on that very deck, and it wasn't long before I let out a long sigh and returned to the familiar story of a distraught dad named Jairus who breathlessly tells Jesus about his 12-year-old daughter who was very sick, trying to recover in their home. His precious girl was so sick that she was near death. As my eyes methodically slid across the words in Luke chapter 8, they did a double take of verse 50 in The Passion Translation:

> *"While Jesus was still speaking ... someone came from Jairus'*
> *house and told him, 'There's no need to bother the Master any*
> *further. Your daughter has passed away. She's gone.' When*
> *Jesus heard this, he turned to Jairus and said, 'Don't yield*
> *to your fear. Have faith in me and she will live again.'"*

"Don't yield to your fear." I hit repeat in my mind: Don't yield to your fear, Sherilyn, don't yield to your fear. The all-too-familiar voice of God's Spirit challenged my spirit. That admonishment began to sass back and chase fear around like an unruly toddler inside me while I pondered what it means to yield to something or someone?

As a verb, yield means "to give way to arguments, demands, or pressure." Whoa! That. Was. Exactly. How. Fear. Was. Behaving. Inside. Me. It argued with the truth I knew. Fear demanded I give it time and attention. It pressed on my heart to feel scared about my present day, and my every tomorrow. Fear never plays fair.

Questions from heaven tumbled into my mind: Was I going to yield to the fear that was trying to choke my faith out or would I fight back? What would I do with this lie from hell that was sounding alarms begging me to yield to fear? Would I permit fear to call the shots or God's truth to do so, no matter how far-fetched that truth seemed in the confusion? On and on the questions tumbled down, challenging me to choose a different way.

> Fear demands I give it time and attention. It presses on my heart to feel scared about my present day, and my every tomorrow. Fear never plays fair.

And there on the deck, as the sun rose high above the condos over the bay, my spirit grabbed ahold of that phrase and my heart did a slow motion 180-flip.

There's always a choice. Every single time, in every single situation, I have a choice, and so do you. It's the choice between standing at attention ready to "obey" the voice of fear or bravely using our very own voice to prophecy to the lie coming against us, and in turn, worship the King of our hearts and lives. I chose the latter that morning (admittedly, I don't always) and something shifted within, granting me courage and wisdom to stand up and face the day and its challenges, and with a restored sense of confidence in the One who knows us most and loves us best.

He alone brings life to the threat of death in and around us! He alone can relate to all the injustice-turned-fear in our unruly circumstances. He alone can fill our heart and minds with peace smack dab in the middle of what feels, or is, terribly unfair.

Life wasn't fair for Jesus either. In fact, His short life on earth was marked by injustice. And we don't have to look any further than the stories that unfold on the pages of both the Old and New Testament to see that life brings injustice to every pair of sandals that walk on earth.

"Jesus was pierced in his side with the spear of man's hatred. Eternal pleasures are found hidden in the wounds of Christ, where Jesus responded to the world's hatred with sacred blood and water flowing from his side. Forgiveness and grace splashed on the dirt. We are now seated with Christ at his right side."
— Notes on Psalm 16 from The Passion Translation in regard to verse 11 [43]

I copied these notes into my personal journal followed by my own handwritten words, "This. Is. Glorious." Because I really do believe it is! Can you spare a minute to hit pause and reread that quote slowly, and then read it again? Give it time to settle in your spirit for just a bit.

We cannot take lightly the response of Jesus to the hatred He met in the world. That response, and His wounds, hold eternal pleasure. I know it can be hard to understand, to believe and accept. Regardless, it's true, and one day we will all be caught up in the glory of its reality.

Whatever is true for Jesus can be true for His followers. Therefore, it's in our forgiveness and surrender to the places of our lives that hold sorrow and injustice where meaning and purpose for this life on earth can be discovered. That's the message of the cross; life is found in resurrection that follows death! Every single time!

Death doesn't have the last word. In the kingdom of heaven, life does! Therefore, with faith, you and I can release and trust that every wrong we endure will be made right because of the power of resurrection that followed the injustice and heartache of the cross. Eternal pleasures are hidden in the wounds inflicted there. All things, even the hard things, are bursting with purpose and hope.

Hallelujah! As disciples of Jesus, we follow the Son of God *and* the Son of Man, fully God *and* fully human. That's a truth we find very hard

Fear demands I give
it time and attention.
It presses on my heart
to feel scared
about my present day
and my every tomorrow.
Fear never plays fair.

to get our finite mind to comprehend. But we must try, for this is the same God who tells us that when we have trouble in the world and face injustice, we can be of good cheer and press forward with courage because the Man of Sorrows has overcome what is broken and dark, at times evil and full of injustice.

There is no disappointment or trouble endured by us that can compare to what Jesus endured as He was despised and rejected, acquainted with grief and suffering. Life wasn't fair for Him either.

Placing Blame

Dave and I were headed not to the ER this time, but to a pain management specialist in hopes that she had some new trick up her sleeve for Dave's severe and chronic leg pain. Just about three years later, and the pain was manifesting different than pseudogout with even more agony and less ability to move freely, seemingly brought on by an afternoon at the golf course. One month turned into two, turned into nine, leaving Pete full of misery and immobility. The pain that started in his lower back would radiate through his hip and down his right leg, making him static without the aid of a walker or a cane, which led to frequent stumbles and falls. Feeling off balance was annoying on its best days. So, once again, my very athletic, very capable husband of 37 years who just 8 months before the golf outing was attending Rock Steady boxing classes 5 days a week, teaching a handful of those very classes, riding his Harley and bicycle, golfing on occasion, and managing our desert landscaped yard. He could no longer navigate any such thing. Our normal radically morphed into an unrecognizable abnormal that we were forced to stare down and adjust to.

Dave's life has been sorely interrupted by challenges and discouragement on a daily basis while my days are riddled with interruptions, and that old "friend," fear, showed up to visit both of us most days screeching within, "This Is SO Unfair!"

*"Faith never knows where it is being led,
but it knows and loves the One who is leading."*
— Oswald Chambers, My Utmost for His Highest [44]

I Don't Deserve This!

There are times for all of us when we are in a crisis that is chronic, one that keeps washing over us like waves in the ocean, and proves that life is absolutely, unequivocally, 110% *unfair*. And there, in our human limitations, we melt down. No one deserves Parkinson's in their body nor their home. You don't deserve your assignment either; the one that brings heartache and unbearable challenges to you and others you love.

Fill-in-the-blank based on your earthly experience: No one deserves _____. And Jesus didn't deserve the cross, to put it mildly. You and I did (Romans 6:23). It's not about what we deserve or don't deserve, it's about all of us encountering tribulation and injustice. No one escapes it. Not even the Son of God and Son of Man. It's about Jesus being resurrected so that we don't have to be imprisoned by the tribulation or the injustice. His resurrection made our tribulation and injustice temporary. We can celebrate that, especially when there is little-to-nothing else to celebrate!

But even with the awareness of that reality, there are times when those who live with chronic pain or chronic crisis just clip. We break, and honesty comes gushing out like a vehement puke of last night's meal in the lap of the person seemingly responsible but isn't. It's not pretty. It's not kind. It's not Jesus-like. It's not easy to pick up the pieces, take the words back. It's impossible to undo a meltdown. And it's not possible to lay our head on the pillow at night as the one who had the meltdown for reasons the other person can't control. But those living with injustice must learn the hard way, like we did at our house, to be comfortable with our humanity, to be in the habit of admitting how desperately we need God in and out of our trouble; it's imperative for survival. And we are desperate for forgiveness to flow freely, offering and receiving it. We must become okay with being human and know that, in our humanity, we have limits. Every last one of us. And that's okay!

In a chronic crisis there will be times when our response is healthy and good but, sadly, there will be other times when it's unhealthy and not helpful and, in fact, hurtful. God is okay with both! God is there for both. He has a well-worn bench where we can collapse after both scenarios play out and eventually settle down and catch our breath because He knows. His Son experienced life on this earth, so He gets that life just isn't fair. And He was clear that Jesus didn't come to earth to do His own will but to live out the will of the One who sent Him (John 6:38). The Father's purpose in every life is that injustice take a back seat and His sovereignty become the catalyst for peace. Proven in the life of His Son on earth.

> *"Whatever game God is playing with human beings and their*
> *suffering; He has played fair in taking his own medicine."*
> *– Dorothy Sayers, The Greater Trumps (Great Chaos?)* [45]

Excessively and Magnificently Good

Trouble. I have it, you have it, they have it. Trouble marks the life of every person on this earthly journey, including that of the Son of God and Son of Man. But Jesus didn't seem to have that chronic longing to avoid or bid his hardship farewell. Instead, He was focused on one thing and that was to do the Father's will (John 6:38), and that included suffering on earth. We all must navigate hardship in life and when we do, it can seem so unfair or in fact, *be* so unfair. It's not until we gaze at the Suffering Jesus who willingly accepted the inequity of His heavenly assignment, that we can hit pause on the injustice we're enduring and catch our breath (Philippians 2:6-8).

In his second letter to the Corinthians, Paul wrote about the trouble we all face throughout our lives explaining that *"our light and momentary troubles are achieving for us an eternal glory that far outweighs them all"*

(2 Corinthians 4:17). Okay, Paul, we get that it's momentary. But light, as in easy, not so much. It almost seems offensive for Paul to refer to our troubles as *light*. That just doesn't always settle in my shipwrecked soul, so I went searching for the reason behind his words. For God's reason. The last phrase of that verse in the original language hints at Paul's rationale as it reads: *a far more exceeding and eternal weight of glory.* The word "exceeding" is the Greek word hyperbole, and literally means "excess."[46]

Let that sit on your heart for just a moment before moving on: *our troubles will one day be exchanged for something excessively and magnificently good.* That's hard to imagine. But enter faith and it becomes a game-changer.

I love words and *hyperbole* is right up there with a few of my favorites. The thought of hyperbole takes me back to my first period freshman English class at Leigh High School. Mr. Mudd was our "old" teacher, likely nearing retirement and probably younger than I am now (smile). He towered over his students and commanded our attention with his deep voice and strong hand on the green chalkboard as he wrote definitions for words, labels for sentence structure and class assignments. I can almost hear Mr. Mudd bellowing across our 14-and 15-year-old heads that hyperbole is "a figure of speech that uses extreme exaggeration to make a point or show emphasis." (I had to read that more than once too.) I immediately liked the word. Hyperbole. I like how it sounds rolling off my tongue. I like its definition. And I like its use in creative writing. Hyperbole. Paul was brilliant. The Holy Spirit is even more so. Therefore, we can be sure that their intentional use of a word in Greek that literally means "exceeding excellency" was meant to be a game-changer. Take that in.

You and I will get an exchange in heaven for our troubles on earth, and it will be more than excellent. That's hard to comprehend. Like really hard, especially when you stand in the middle of a mess that is causing so much trouble and turning quickly into hardship and can feel so unfair!

Another meaning for the Greek word hyperbole is "out of measure." So, this endless glory that one day replaces the troubles we have endured on earth is too weighty to even measure and exceeds excellence as we know it!! I love this promise! It means that I can allow the "far more exceeding eternal weight of glory" to revamp my perspective toward the trouble and injustice I face, or that of someone I love, whether it's minimal, monumental, or somewhere in between. My trouble, and your trouble, is on mission to achieve, design, or fully accomplish for us, an eternal weight of glory. Eternal is forever. Weight implies that it's heavy, as in significant.

Glory can be defined as the sum total of God's goodness. Holy wow! Trouble is for us and not against us. It has purpose and is glad to cooperate with heaven while on earth to prepare something unspeakably good for each one of us!

- Let *that* speak to the trouble you're enduring.
- Let *that* tell your heart and mind what to think about the trouble you're standing in.
- Let *that* very promise settle your heart and instruct your mind.

Paul is writing about a mind-blowing change of perspective for the injustice that welcomes trouble, not about our circumstances! I need it, you need it, they need it. We all need a life hack for this thing called trouble and its injustice in any set of circumstances. Thanks to Paul – to God – we now have one. The sense of unfairness in the hardship we've been assigned just got a little bit lighter and less overwhelming to navigate. Consider pausing to read the first few sentences of this paragraph out loud emphasizing the word, "that" a little more each time in an effort to catch your breath before tomorrow's sunrise.

BREATHE DEEPLY

"Breathing is not only the process of inhaling and exhaling,
it's a reminder that every breath we take is a gift of life."
— Author Unknown

INHALE

Psalm 89:13-18
Isaiah 53:1-7
Mark 4:21-25
Hebrews 4:14-16

EXHALE

♦ Choose a verse, a sentence or just a phrase from one of the passages above.[47]

♦ Write it down on something you can post in your home, office or car, or at least carry with you.

♦ Meditate on its meaning; think about it again and again (and again!) over the course of your day/week.

♦ Read it in context.

♦ Read it in other Bible versions; the Amplified and Passion Translation are favorites.

♦ Look up the meaning of the words that you want to better understand.

♦ Memorize the verse or passage.

♦ Let the verse or phrase run around on the inside of you until it becomes your very own, part of your DNA.

♦ Consider personalizing it by inserting your name, or praying it for yourself, someone else, or for a situation.

nine
WEARY

"Jesus said, 'Come to Me, all of you who are weary and carry heavy burdens, and I will give you rest.'"

<small>MATTHEW 11:28 NLT</small>

Someone once said the hardest thing about life is that it's so daily. They weren't wrong. A circumstance or a relationship can hurt with a word, a glance, a text. The pain starts tapping on the door of our mind with the steadiness of a leaky faucet as a recurring thought ushers in disappointment.

It's easy to become agitated and try to fix something or change someone in an effort to make life better, or at least try to make things return to the way they were. There's a longing in the distress of such moments that keeps circling back around sounding something like, "Not this again. Please life situation, or so-and-so, go back to what I know. Please just stay the same. Don't do this. Don't do that."

We know what to do with the familiar, how to navigate those situations and people we know well, even when surrounded by unhealthy patterns. And, all the while, we long for change. A different outcome. Something better.

Ultimately, comfort is what we're after and disappointment makes us uncomfortable. Trying to fix a situation or change another person may yield dividends for a time, but when it repeatedly falls short, we're left discouraged, something we all struggle to avoid at all costs. I mean, who likes to be discouraged, right? It's a downer and can cloud our days with heartache and weariness. Discouragement feeds weariness tempting us to give up or, at best, try to silence the broken record. So, we try harder, seek to be better, go at it again, only to be met with the same.

The cycle of weariness is exhausting. Yet, even in exhaustion, we strive to do good, be good, think good thoughts, believe good things, try harder or try another way. We tire ourselves out again and again. The battle is real in the do-good-be-good fight, as we seek it over and over and over while getting nothing in return. Or even worse, when rejection or judgment, mistreatment or misunderstanding ricochet off our soul leaving us holding the same old issue, feeling perplexed one more time. That's when it takes a turn and seems like an impossible fight as the weariness of well doing sets in like powdered Jello without enough water added to the mix (Galatians 6:9). Soon we're smack dab in the middle of a cycle of doing good and feeling disheartened, doing good and feeling disheartened, doing good and ... you know the drill. Weariness is fatigue-turned-exhaustion in real time. We seek to please others, and often rightly so, but rarely does that work. Not for the long haul.

A dear friend of mine is known for the wisdom that comes from her lips. She often says she would rather be on the Potter's wheel than the people's wheel. And for a recovered people pleaser, she knows what she's talking about! There may be nothing quite as wearisome as trying to please someone else because, ultimately, much like multitasking, it's an illusion. You and I simply cannot please anyone all the time. We can't even please some of the people some of the time. You've probably already discovered that.

Even when our houses are laced with Bible verses and our knees sore from praying, we can slip deeper and deeper into discouragement which, over time, will cause us to face-plant into weariness before we know what knocked us over. Weariness makes us lose heart, and sometimes hope. When we're able to turn our heads, there in the dirt, we will likely notice that we're lying in a valley called trouble where weariness thrives.

The Valley of Trouble

The Israelites had their fair share of trouble. I think they would admit that the struggle is real. God's chosen people knew trouble like an old friend, up close and personal. They wore their own weariness on their sleeve, letting their circumstances in the wilderness bring out the worst in them. They were known for their bad attitudes, constantly grumbling and complaining (Exodus 16:2-3).

The books of the Old Testament are like tattered journal pages packed full of life lessons that involve victorious battles and overwhelming difficulties. In them, we read how the Israelites faced weariness head on in real time. Those early books recount stories that are, at times, disturbing and yet act as a reliable reflection of the relentless trouble God's people faced, and the serious weariness they felt.

In one of the more unsettling Old Testament accounts, there is a literal Valley of Trouble known as the Valley of Achor. Achor in Hebrew means "troubled."[48] The account of what happened in The Valley of Achor is a hard story to read, let alone swallow (Joshua 7). But it's true, and it's sobering, and it took place under the Old Covenant of Law. As God's people, we now live under the New Covenant of Grace (Jeremiah 31:31-34;

Romans 6:14), but we still glean instruction and revelation from the wandering journey of God's people in the wilderness. They often landed face first in the Valley of Trouble where God rescued their weary souls over and over again.

I've camped in the Valley of Trouble many more times than I care to count, and I hate camping! Likely, you have too. And every single time you or I arrive at our camp site, we desperately hold out hope that our stay (or face-plant) will be short-lived. As brief as possible. Yet often, moments in the Valley of Trouble have a peculiar way of turning into hours that become days, spreading into weeks that are soon marked by months, and sometimes even years.

I can tell you that every single time my circumstantial trip took me to a new valley, or forced me to revisit an old one, I did *not* want to be there. I'm sure you can relate! Weariness gains momentum as the clock ticks and tocks in the valley, and hopelessness can become lodged in our weary hearts while there. Every visit would find me hoping and praying (begging) that I wouldn't be there long, that I could cut a break just as soon as the trouble ended. Inevitably, I'd end up pitching a tent and staying awhile. Trouble is like that, relentless. And in those moments turned hours, days, weeks, even months and sometimes, years, we wonder if the Lord is *still* good because the dusty nature in the Valley of Trouble makes us doubt that reality.

The Valley of Trouble is never a chosen, desired vacation spot. And certainly not a place where we hope to take up residence or get stuck. In fact, we don't want to be in the valley at all, so we start looking for a way to fix something or control someone or, better yet, come up with a plan to hike out as fast as we can! And if you're like me, and King David, once you realize you might be there awhile, you feel desperate to taste and see that the Lord is *still* good because it doesn't feel like He is! It doesn't look like He is. It's hard to believe He is!

It's in the Valley of Achor where we find ourselves feasting on disappointment while toying with the idea of giving up all together. That's the nature of trouble; it attracts discouragement and hopelessness while its victim is still scratching their head trying to figure out exactly what happened. The burden and confusion become heavier and heavier while weariness sets in, and we grow increasingly more desperate for answers from heaven, especially the longer our stay in the valley lasts.

The Solace of a Mobile Sanctuary

I've developed an odd sort of habit over the years that serves me and those close to me well, however strange it may be. I find it helps relieve tension that can settle into any given situation or relationship as a result of trying to please someone, communicate or resolve conflict. Have you ever noticed how easy it is to get along with everybody when you're at home alone? Sigh. When I find myself frustrated, unable to reach resolution with another person or in any given situation, when I start to go down the path that I know leads to weariness, I head straight for the key rack in our home in order to indulge in this crazy habit of driving alone in my car, somewhat aimlessly.

Any vehicle can become a sanctuary, and driving solo can have a medicinal effect on body, soul and spirit. The make of the car and the destination hold no importance. It's the solace and temporary sneaking away from reality to ward off weariness that matters. It's as if an unconventional place and the confines of a car are an invitation to reflect on my thoughts and commune with the One who knows me best and loves me most. Those times in my sacred automobile allow me to let my guard down and lay my heart bare before God. The car can fill with loud prayers, the shouting of frustrations, and on occasion, gentle weeping on the way back home. Any and all expressions of pouring out my heart before God is acceptable as I steer my vehicle down any given road (Psalms 62:8). I am prone to save the shouting and cry fests for my nocturnal getaways because, well, you can imagine the looks I get.

Therapeutic drives have permitted me to keep an uncluttered soul and weariness in check. Clutter can be defined as "a pile of stuff in a disordered state."[49] Internal clutter is no different. It can pile up within us and readily choke out joy, courage, peace, forgiveness, victory, faith. It drains our energy and keeps us busy shuffling stacks of discouragement, fear, anxiety, unforgiveness, bitterness and resentment from place to place, never finding space to sit and rest. Soul clutter obstructs our view from the thing that God has on his heart for us in the now moment. In short, the clutter of the soul keeps weariness alive.

Clearing Out the Piles

The bedrock for creating an uncluttered soul is keeping short accounts with God and with others. It's showing up with a willingness to keep the door open to the new and the different, forgiveness or the unexpected miracle and the hopeful future. So, whether your new SUV or your beat up old sedan is a sanctuary doesn't matter. The place makes no difference. It's the priority of stepping away and choosing to be authentic in His Presence that makes the difference. It's about a space and a habit created as a safe place where you can go to be stripped bare before God, conveying the truth of your inner self, even *to* yourself. I still take a solo drive at times but, in more recent years, I tend to stay home and plop down in what I call my heaven on earth chair; a big easy chair with an ottoman dedicated to times spent with the Father, Son and Holy Spirit when weariness is chomping at my soul.

> **The clutter of the soul keeps weariness alive.**

Weariness is the warning light on the dashboard of our lives indicating that you and I are desperate for time with God and have a high need for respite. We all need a space where we can be reminded that this world is not our home, and what we're going through simply can't be compared to the "coming glory" because, the reality for all of us is, weariness is a part of our earthly journey (Romans 8:18). And Jesus was clear about its antidote:

presence. The remedy for our weariness is His Presence. Jesus invites you and me to bring our heavy hearts and many cares into His Presence where we can find renewal and blessed quiet for our souls. There we join Him who promises that His burden is light and easy to bear (Matthew 11:28, 30 AMP).

We will find few more comforting verses in the Bible than Matthew 11:28. Maybe none more hopeful for you and me, the weary ones. Jesus invited His disciples (us) to come after Him, to follow Him (Matthew 16:24). He invited them to come with Him to a solitary place (Mark 6:31). They were asked to pray and wait with Him as He was about to face His darkest hour. But only the weary, those parched of soul, and little children, are invited to come *to Him* (Mark 10:14-5; John 7:37). Pause and sit with that for a minute. There is something deeply personal about this holy invitation for the vulnerable, the needy, those who can't help themselves.

The word for "weary" in the original language is labor. In Greek it literally means to feel fatigued, tired out from hard work, toil.[50] Navigating trouble, hardship, disappointment, and heartache is toil, it's exhausting, wearisome. As is loving well, communicating, and getting along with others, forgiving, and choosing to believe the best in them. This is the hard work of our lives. At times, very hard. When we are at it on the long haul, feeling worn out, each weary breath will whisper into our soul that the situation most important to us, the one always on our mind and ever in our prayers, is hopeless and beyond repair. This holy invitation to *come to Him* is for those very moments and seasons. We are invited, encouraged, summoned if you will, to come to Jesus. He is kind, gentle and humble, and He has rest on His heart for ours.

However, don't mistake His kind, gentle, humble ways for being weak, delicate or unable to speak up. Just a quick read through the gospel books and you'll know what I mean. Being tethered to Him can help life feel less demanding, and what He asks of us is far less complicated than what we ask of ourselves. His Presence brings ease, relief, and repair to our tired, weary souls.

Sitting down to catch your breath in a season of weariness is not a one-and-done practice. It puts a stop to the crazy swirling in our heads that is meant to slow us down long enough to let our hearts grow soft, pliable, willing. Therefore, it's to our benefit to do it often. Finding a bench, literally or metaphorically, to sit with the One who has overcome the world (subdued its power in our circumstance) is a good practice. It's vital and necessary for this journey we call faith. It's there on the bench where heaven meets earth, and it's there that we are changed, even when life feels heavy and hard and isn't fair. At least not here, not now. In fact, at times, life doesn't even make sense in a season of trouble and heartache. But when we pause to catch our breath, the Spirit of the Living God helps us press on regardless of the shifting circumstances around us.

When it's hard, He is there. And when He's there, our soul can rest. Truly rest. It's worth the time and discipline to slow down and remember that Jesus invites you and me to sit *with Him* to be refreshed and repaired. He suffered. He felt deep heartache. He endured for *the joy* set before Him, His joy was our freedom (Hebrews 12:2).

> *"Come to Me, all you who are weary and carry heavy*
> *burdens, and I will give you rest. Take My yoke upon*
> *you. Let Me teach you, because I am humble and*
> *gentle at heart, and you will find rest for your*
> *souls. For My yoke is easy to bear,*
> *and the burden I give you is light."*
> *– Jesus (Matthew 11:28-30 NLT)*

Jesus bids us come, to be with Him. Don't you appreciate how uncomplicated and direct that is? His words are such a welcome invitation. In fact, so much so that it feels more like a sigh of relief for our disappointed and hurting souls than a request.

I've always thought that God's favorite word just might be "come." You can look in Scripture for yourself to see how many times Father, Son or Holy Spirit say, "come" on the pages of their story. Our story. We can't help but hear the tenderness and empathy in the voice of Jesus as He calmly says, *"Come to Me weary one, you can yoke up with Me."* And yet, do you, like me, hear a strangeness to that offer, just the same?

The "be connected to Jesus" part sounds familiar enough, but the yoke sounds a little odd or, at best, unfamiliar. However, it would have made perfect sense to the people Jesus was talking to that day. Yokes were part of their village experience. They got it. They knew about the significance of yoked oxen ploughing in a field. They would have known that a yoke was made to fit each ox individually.

The oxbow was made of wood or metal and fitted to the neck size of each ox. The two oxbows were never the same size because one ox was always meant to lead and, you guessed it, the other was to follow. The lead ox was typically older and larger so that it was able to take the younger, smaller ox where they both needed to go while pulling the greater weight.

"Two oxen are chosen to share a yoke. The first is an older seasoned ox. He is trained and hardy from years of routine. The second is a new young ox. He has potential but is inexperienced. By sharing the same yoke with a veteran workhorse, the elder trains the young. Not only that, but the experienced one draws harder to bear the majority of the load. Since the older one leads, the younger ox does not have to wonder what to do."[51]
– Brannon Deibert

The purpose of a yoke is to allow two animals to *move together* to accomplish the same thing. But you can imagine that it only works if one ox can lead and the other follows. It's a compelling analogy as it relates to being discouraged, weary, or heavy-laden, as the original language states in Matthew 11. The invitation is to our discouraged and weary self as Jesus gently whispers, "Will you let me lead?" And we respond with gusto, "Absolutely, Lord!" And we mean it. Until the Valley of Trouble begins to close in on us after dwelling there for a long time, and then all religious bets are off!

When things spin out of control … for the first time or the 83rd time … our default and seeming need to control veers off the charts! We presume that if we can control the chaos around us, then surely, we can control the chaos within us.

The Need to Control

Holy Spirit pressed on my heart to answer the question: How's that working for you? In other words - does trying to control the chaos in your outside world help bring peace to your inside world? I've had to acknowledge many times over that control just wasn't working great for me. Not really. I have a hunch you can relate.

Feeling overwhelmed and weary on the inside can ignite within us a desperate need to try to control the outside. Control does little more than frustrate us and those around us; the ones who are trying their best to navigate trouble too. It becomes apparent that our most valiant efforts to control others, and situations, don't cultivate the peace or joy we're after. We try with vigorous effort to fix situations for people, and sometimes we attempt to fix people. But it never works. At least not permanently. As we seek to control people and situations, discouragement starts gaining traction and soon it overtakes us, arresting our hearts and leaving us weary. The Valley of Trouble is obliged to assist us in seeing the value of raising the white flag of surrender and declaring what has proven true time and time again; control is an illusion.

What diminishes a desperate need to control, that default within that pushes us deeper into weariness and makes those around us miserable, is to lean into the invitation of Jesus to come. When we listen, not so much with our ears but with our spirit, as Jesus ever so tenderly and yet, relentlessly, persuades us to yoke up with Him and choose the smaller oxbow; that choice alters the valley landscape and lets us breathe again.

And if we'll wait for it, Jesus will always add something that soothes our anxious thoughts and feelings – *"Come learn of Me, for I am gentle and lowly of heart ..."*

"Gentle and lowly." Of all the things Jesus, the Son of Man *and* Son of God could have said about Himself, He chose gentle (mild, kind, tender) and lowly (humble, low in status and importance). In his heart-transforming work, *Gentle and Lowly; The Heart of Christ for Sinners and Sufferers*, Dane Ortland unpacks the "gentle and lowly" nature of Jesus in his opening chapter as he describes the innate nature of the Son of God:

> *"Meek. Humble. Gentle. Jesus is not trigger-happy. Not harsh, reactionary, easily exasperated. He's the most understanding person in the universe. The posture most natural to him is not a pointed finger, but open arms. The point in saying that Jesus is lowly is that he is accessible ... no one in human history has ever been more approachable than Jesus Christ. No prerequisites. No hoops to jump through. You don't need to unburden or collect yourself and then come to Jesus. Your very burden is what qualifies you to come. 'Gentle and lowly.' This, according to his own testimony, is Christ's very heart. This is who he is. Tender. Open. Welcoming. Accommodating. Understanding. Willing. Lowly gentleness is not one way Jesus occasionally acts towards others. Gentleness is who he is. It is his heart. He cannot un-gentle himself toward his own any more than you and I can change our eye color. It's who we are."[52]*

Jesus didn't say, "Come and learn of Me, for I am majestic or powerful, holy or sovereign" even though He is. He didn't say, "Come and learn of Me, for I am harsh or judgmental, shaming or punitive" which He is not, although often accused of. We can become increasingly more and more grateful and comforted by His invitation to learn from His gentleness and humility. So, when we say yes to His invitation and yoke up with the gentle and humble One, letting go of our seeming desperate need to control and, instead, follow His lead, we find that we're able to catch our breath and settle. We exhale to release the disappointment and heartache that makes us weary. We inhale to receive His Presence and hope in all things made right. One day. And there we begin to let our weary soul rest as we release our discouragement and cling to His hope. We may not fully understand it but, man, do we need it! Each and every one of us desperately need it!

Presence is the only transformative solution for soul weariness. It's in His Presence where we gain insight into who we are in the now moment and who we can become in the next moment. It's where the healing heart of the Father offers solace, and the helping hand of the Spirit clears the clutter within. The weariness in our soul will begin to dissipate as you and I go to Jesus, whether by way of an aimless drive, getting comfortable in an easy chair, taking a walk on a favored trail in the woods or along the shore, or some other place reserved for you and me to linger with Him. It's there that we can eventually catch our breath and find strength to trust once again in the One who knows us best and loves us most.

> *"What does the Lord want from me? A deep seated Yes!"*
> *– Mother Basilea Schlink*[53]

A Modern Day Parable About Presence

October is a glorious month in central Pennsylvania. Trees are copious with vibrant orange, brilliant red, and glorious golden leaves. One must see it in real time to truly appreciate its magnificence. My late brother, Ron, lived on the west coast but loved fall on the east coast so he planned a trip to see my family and the majestic central Pennsylvania fall one last time. That visit came and went quickly and, as it came to an end, it was unusually bittersweet. Bitter because I knew it would be the last time I would see my dear brother face-to-face on earth. Bitter with that unexplainable and inexpressible "knowing" that this is the final hour when death seems to be knocking on the door of someone's life whom you deeply love and thoroughly enjoy. And sweet because our time together had been. But Ron was so tired and had grown so uncomfortable in his weak and failing body which offered a sweetness in knowing he would soon return to the comfort of his own home. My brother was tired. Very, very tired. My brother was weary.

I told Ron that I'd not be going to the airport with him that day. That was out of character for me, so I knew I needed to explain. We talked at great length about airports and goodbyes and what they both still did to my inner person after years and years of unbearable sadness for me when the two intersected. Airports and goodbyes had painfully crisscrossed over and over again for me through the years of growing up. Airports and goodbyes were second nature to me. I would say goodbye to my mother and the large, blended family with whom I spent most of my time in California on one end of any given holiday and then say goodbye to my daddy and his small family in Arizona on the other.

I'm not sure why, but I even retold Ron stories about some of the heart-wrenching goodbyes I had lived through with non-family members, all taking place in an airport somewhere. Those stories caught Ron off-guard. He and I had shared our hearts candidly and intimately over the years as many siblings do when they cling to one another after family security is threatened or remains weak. Ron expressed his amazement that there were still things unknown between us that held such significance. I gently explained that I simply could not bear the pain of watching him board a plane for a separation that was likely going to be permanent this time. I did not reveal that a bit of my hesitation was also in the heartache I felt watching him force a smile and act as if he was feeling okay when I knew he was in unbearable pain from the escalating symptoms of the AIDS virus that was draining earthly life from his weakened body.

I was convinced that, to watch his frail body slowly board an airplane that was going to demand so many hours of his day traveling, knowing he had spent most of his time in bed during his visit with my family would truly be intolerable for me. And all because he wanted to visit us one more time before he left earth. Ron had purposed in his heart to return to Pennsylvania to be with me and my family of boys one last time, and he did it! Mission accomplished. I couldn't help but wonder if this would be the last big mission of his earthly life. Soon I would find out that, indeed, it would be.

We sat mostly in silence that dreary day in the dim light of our paternal grandmother's antique lamp. Our lips spoke little while our tears flowed freely. Ron was weak and weary, and so was his baby sister. And yet there was a strength that was stirred by being with one another. Ron had been bravely fighting a battle of deteriorating health for over 10 years, he was tired. Very, very tired. My dear brother was weary. I had been steadfastly fighting a battle of faith against the plans of the enemy for Ron's life and was also tired. In that moment I wanted to be sure that Ron was sure he would be in heaven after he took his last breath. So, I gently asked what I had asked him many times before: "Ron, do you believe in your heart and are you willing to say that Jesus is Lord? Are you sure you'll be in heaven when I get there?" With weariness and weakness in his voice, but strength and assurance in his spirit, he whispered: "I'm sure. I'll see you on the other side. Jesus is Lord" (Romans 10:9-10).

> **Presence is always the remedy for a weary heart.**

As we sat together in the stillness, Ron mustered the strength to reiterate how much he loved me and how much my love had affected him. He spoke while tears trickled down his prominent cheekbones, which was very much out of character for him. Not the tender part, the crying part. Soon his words came to a halt and, when they did, he stood with arduous energy to hug me. I knew this was goodbye, and I thought my heart would pound right through my clothing and my spirit would faint within me.

He pushed out another labored breath and struggled a bit to leave his chair and move toward me. We hugged for what seemed an eternity as my

Presence

is always the
remedy for a weary
heart.

sobs became more pronounced with each minute. He kissed my forehead, looked deep into my eyes, and smiled sweetly at me as I tried to contain my convulsive crying. David came in and gently reminded us that it was past time to leave. David held me as Ron made his way to the van, walking slowly and weeping gently but always doing what had to be done.

That was the last time I saw my brother in person. He passed peacefully in his San Francisco home on Potrero Hill Friday afternoon, just four days after Christmas, and arrived in his heavenly home where I know I'll see him again one day. Even with the assurance of His whereabouts beyond his last breath, his loss created a deep and chronic ache within me that will remain until we are reunited again. He had made it to my home to be with my family one last time. My dear brother traveled all the way across the country to be in the presence of my family to soothe his aching, weary heart. Little did he know that his effort to make the all-day trek by air and back would soothe my aching, weary heart as well.

Presence is always the remedy for a weary heart. People matter, particularly when we're weary, but I'm not convinced any of us can fully catch our breath without spending time in the Presence of Jesus, and nothing may be as exhausting as going at this thing called life, alone.

*If you don't know Jesus personally and are not yet a Christ follower but you want to be, do the following:

1. Simply admit that you need Him in your life and thank Him for dying on the cross to pay the penalty for your sins so that you can be made right with Him. (Talk to Jesus just like you would a friend, there's really nothing more to it.)
2. Acknowledge that He rose from the dead after He was crucified, overcoming death so that you can be born again.
3. PRAY: "Jesus, I believe that you died to take away my sins and adopt me as a son/daughter. I receive the gift of salvation by Your

grace and my faith. I want you to be my Lord, so I give You my heart and life forever. I choose this day to follow You for the rest of my life."

4. Read the following verses: Matthew 16:26; John 1:12-13; John 3:1-6 and 16-18; Romans 6:23; Ephesians 2:4-10

5. Tell another follower of Jesus that you prayed this prayer and send me an email too! I'd love to celebrate your new faith in Christ! (1 Corinthians 5:17-18)

BREATHE DEEPLY

"When we inhale, by prayer, we receive the fresh air of the Holy Spirit.
When we exhale the same air, we announce
Jesus Christ risen by the same Spirit."
– Pope Francis

INHALE

Psalm 23

Psalm 139:1-18

Matthew 11:28-30

Romans 8 (read in The Passion Translation if possible)

EXHALE

- Choose a verse, a sentence or just a phrase from one of the passages above.[54]
- Write it down on something you can post in your home, office or car, or at least carry with you.
- Meditate on its meaning; think about it again and again (and again!) over the course of your day/week.
- Read it in context.
- Read it in other Bible versions; the Amplified and Passion Translation are favorites.
- Look up the meaning of the words that you want to better understand.
- Memorize the verse or passage.
- Let the verse or phrase run around on the inside of you until it becomes your very own, part of your DNA.
- Consider personalizing it by inserting your name, or praying it for yourself, someone else, or for a situation.

ten
BRAVE

"I leave the gift of peace with you - My peace. Not the kind of fragile peace given by the world, but My perfect peace. Don't yield to fear or be troubled in your hearts — instead, be courageous."

– Jesus (John 14:27 TPT)

mpending change of any kind can arrest one's heart and send a mind spinning out of control with legitimate concern, keeping courage at bay. Jesus incited us as His disciples to *"be courageous because He has overcome the world"* (John 16:33). His part is done. He has overcome, subdued the powerful darkness in the world we live in, and victory is promised. Our part is ongoing. We have become brave because we know victory has the final word. Our Savior has rescue on His mind for each one of us. And not just one time at salvation, but over and over again like a watchful lifeguard looking for one struggling who needs help.

Fear is a Bully

Do you ever wake up in the middle of the night struck by fear or a general sense of panic? I do, and I'm not a worrier by nature. But the enemy of our soul comes against our mind night and day. I remember well the mental distress that kept me awake when all around me boxes were piling up and barren walls were staring back at me as we prepared to leave our house-turned-home over more than two decades. The furniture and home decor we sold was going out the door with strangers by the day.

Dismantling a home where a family life thrived for 24 years can evoke serious fear and sure anxiety. The sold sign stood dutifully on our front lawn announcing our impending departure while inside our house we prepared to pull out of the driveway for the last time. The long trek across country would take us to a brand-new life packed full of unknowns. I was not feeling brave, more like intimidated with a hint of grief setting in. There were too many moments to count that held an overwhelming sense of dread amidst the eager anticipation.

The middle-of-the-night (or day) panic-stricken-flashes can reach near habitual status when change is looming. A big change in particular. Such fear begs that we succumb to the temptation to worry instead of trust, and to fret as we stand in the middle of what was, and what is yet to be. We can't always do much about waking up in the middle of the night nor can we always stop the momentary panic of daytime. But the Helper will assist us in restraining our fears and keep them from consuming us (Malachi 3:6). We can call brave up to the surface of our souls and press on.

Fear is a bully that threatens to harm and alter our plans, steal our peace, and shove us around until we're backed into a corner, scared and overwhelmed. Confronting this bully who has an uncanny way of showing up unannounced … in the middle of the day or night … in the middle the unexpected news … in the middle of a conversation … in the middle of anything … is imperative. Bullies thrive on the surprise factor because intimidation is their jam. Every victim of every bully is desperate for a safe place to run out of their reach. I know. I had to contend with a bully in the orchard across the street from my elementary school.

Standing Up to the Bully

Ethan was a bully. My sister and I, along with our neighborhood friends, were often terrorized on our way home from Alta Vista School. I can't remember Ethan Baker's face nor his words, but I'll never forget the fear he evoked in us. Words have power and Ethan's were used to drain bravery from my little girl veins right there in the orchard on more after school walk-throughs than I care to count. But I soon discovered that my words had power too, I just had to use them.

My older sister, Janie, advised me to say the opposite of whatever Ethan said to us, and to say it loud and proud. That's when the habitual scenario changed. When Ethan said: I'm going to trip you and make you fall down! (Gigantic threat I know but remember, I was very young.) I would timidly reply: You are NOT going to trip me, Ethan Baker! I'm NOT going to fall down! (Much better strategy than crying. Ask me how I know.) My short little legs would shake with the faint beat of my shaky voice. But I said it scared, and things changed. It wasn't loud and proud but when I used my words, Ethan lost his. Soon he found another victim or gave up being a bully. I can't recall that part of the story. I sure hope it was the latter.

Using my words held power (Proverbs 18:21). It's no different for you. We can hush the lies that come from the bully of our souls by retaliating with God's truth. Once fear is convinced you and I are not intimidated, it turns to exit the building, or leaves the orchard, because that's the way of a bully. Their game is to threaten and frighten. When their victim speaks up with brave words, even if they're still shaking in their little boots, bullies tend to scamper away.

Satan is a bully. The Word of God is a weapon, and His Spirit adds power to each word spoken, especially out loud.

"We are strongest when we realize that we need the Holy Spirit's help for everything from our breathing to our believing."[55]
— Liberty Savard, Shattering Your Strongholds

The enemy of our soul is called out as an accuser in the last book of the New Testament. He and his helpers (demons) are bullies, and we shut them up and send them scurrying by speaking out what God has done, and what He will do again (Revelation 12:10-11).

Get a Verse

God's words in our mouth become discouragement in the enemy's ear. God's words make us brave. When fear is nipping at your ankles or maybe worse, shrieking in your ears, try this:

- Grab your Bible and search for verses and promises that confirm His truth.
- Look up verses with words like trust, comfort, strength, help.
- Read until your eyes land on something about God that you need; something about Him that comforts your anxious heart, something that brings a pause and ushers in courage and hope.
- Focus your attention on that, focus on Him.
- Sit with Jesus and a blank page.
- Listen and write what you hear Him say to your heart. If it doesn't contradict Scripture, trust it's Him speaking to you!

> **Jesus is the Word. What is needed to be brave is found in what He speaks.**

His words uphold the entire universe day-after-day-after-day, so you and I can rest assured those promises are capable of responding to our needs. His words affect each and every circumstance we face, making us strong and able and brave! Jesus creates what we need out of the resources of heaven, and He often does that by speaking.

Trust His words. Speak them out loud. As you do, courage will rise up in you. His very words will begin to influence whatever concerns you. What Jesus speaks in the invisible realm can give birth to the things you need in the visible. Pay attention with expectation. Jesus is the Word and what is needed in order to be brave is found in what He speaks. Focus your attention on a promise by reading it in multiple versions of the Bible. Write that promise down. Pray it with your own name inserted or that of the one you're praying for. Meditate on each word of that promise.

In other words, get a Bible verse for every fear you face and every trouble you endure! Habitually tell yourself, and others, to "get a verse" and when you do, or they do, it won't be long before you notice your mind begins to quiet down, your body begins to decompress, and your heart begins to feel strong again, able to endure. His words will help you catch your breath. And soon, you will begin to feel more confident, and braver than you did yesterday.

The Working Shelf at God's Desk

Although I'd been teaching for nearly 8 years, I was a new teacher at Sliding Rock Elementary School. I was becoming familiar with the names of the students in my second grade class as I made name tags, marked cubbies, and prepared workbooks. I was also accustomed to fellow teachers "warning" new teachers of challenging students; a rite of passage for new teachers that I was never particularly fond of. Sure enough, Sliding Rock's second grade staff was no different, and seven-year-old, Philip Reece, was no exception.

As a matter of fact, more than one colleague stopped by room 17 to give me the lowdown on what I could expect on the first day, and every day of the school year, in fact, from little Mr. Reece. Unbeknownst to anyone else, I had already requested that the school principal, Ms. Vasquez, assign the "naughty" boys to my class roster because I sincerely love the rambunctious ones who are full of life and energy. I know teachers aren't supposed to have favorite students but those are the students that quickly and typically became my favorites, although I never told a soul. The teachers filled me in about all the things that Philip couldn't do, shouldn't do, and wouldn't do. No one mentioned anything positive about Philip, nor did they think to tell me the most significant reasons he had been retained in first grade. It was the death of his mother during Philip's first grade year. I eventually found out from his dad that Philip didn't "deal well" with his mother's death, and his school life suffered accordingly.

Philip was a very handsome, very tall and very rambunctious freckle-faced boy whose smile melted my heart. I loved Philip from the first day I met him, and every day after the start of that school year. It took me all of about five minutes the first morning to figure out that Philip was indeed going to live up to his reputation described to me. Philip let me know quickly and emphatically that he agreed with the other teachers, he couldn't do the academic work expected of him, he wouldn't be nice on the playground, and he wasn't clear about personal boundaries or socially acceptable expectations. I reminded him quickly and emphatically that I was there to help him learn how to do all of the above, and to do it well. I assured him that I was happy to take full responsibility for his success in my classroom, and on the school grounds.

Philip learned that Mrs. Jameson said what she meant and meant what she said. He spent most of his recess time standing by my side and most of the school hours sitting by my desk. Sure enough, in good time, Philip and I began to love and respect one another just as I had anticipated.

I had a vintage teacher's desk in this particular classroom with a small pull-out shelf beside my desk chair for additional workspace. Somehow that became Philip's "desk of choice" for most of his hours at school. It was no different on a particular day about mid-year when my work was interrupted by Philip's fixed gaze on me just before that he said something astounding. I broke his stare by looking over at him as he stepped even closer to me. I was sitting and he was standing, making our position eyeball to eyeball. Philip inquired, "You know what Mrs. Jameson?" Before I could reply, he answered his own question pronouncing proudly, "You smell like my mama!" There was a pregnant pause. Dumbfounded by Philip's words, and with what felt like a grapefruit size lump in my throat, tears glistened in my eyes as I wrapped that dear boy in a great big bear hug. Soon the world started spinning again as he and I worked together on the academic issue throwing him a curveball, and our school day pressed on. But his words. Oh my.

Those words offered as a gift echoed in the hallway of my heart for what seemed like an eternity. Slow as molasses, his private announcement (compliment!) began to make sense; Philip Reece didn't smell his mama on my skin, he felt the love of his mama in my heart. And that love made him brave enough to consider recreating who he was going to be. Brave enough to try again, change his attitude, alter his actions. Love makes us brave. Love calls courage to the surface of our soul.

I've treasured that sacred moment in my heart for many years and tried to track Philip down upon our return to Arizona. Sadly, his sister told me that her tall, handsome brother had passed. I had waited too long. I regret that very much. And I am forever thankful for the memory and the image it gives of God inviting you and me to His desk where, in essence, He pulls out a working shelf when we need to be close to Him. There in that intimate space, He never gives credence to where we've been, how we've messed up, what others are saying about us, or how desperately we need help. Instead, His attention and heart of compassion is fixed firmly on you or me, the one struggling the most in this classroom called life. And like a tired, heartbroken seven-year-old who had lost the love of his mama, his sense of security and so much more, we too can stay right next to the Father for as long as we need to, as long as we want to. He invites us to come close. He will be there, close to us in our own hardships and troubles (James 4:8a).

It's in our longing for life to improve where the scent of His lovingkindness can heal and influence the pain of our soul. He is heartbroken over what has broken our hearts. He has heard and seen all that has happened to you and to me, how life has beaten us up and how grief has torn us down. He cares and longs to draw close so that His grace can soothe and heal our anxious thoughts. He's intent upon us hearing His bidding to come close

> **Love calls courage to the surface of our soul.**

so that He can help us and heal us and make brave again. So, we hold space for God and receive what He offers.

Philip had to trust me and believe what I told him, especially about himself. We, too, are needy, dependent students in God's classroom, and it's in standing at His desk, close to Him, where our longings can be satisfied, and our empty hearts replenished. That's His promise and He's good for His word. His love can call courage up in every one of us. You are braver than you think because God's love is greater than you know.

His love makes us brave (1 John 4:18).

God's Love is Different

Her love had failed me. Her words bruised and wounded my soul. Someone I should have been able to trust to love and protect me used her voice to judge and criticize me. Her disapproval of me revealed the depth of pain in her. She was conniving at times, hurt my feelings often and rejected who I was with added pressure to be who she wanted me to be. Ultimately, the love I gave her was not returned. Her love let me down. Her inadequacies born in her brokenness failed me.

God's love, attached to His promises, isn't like that. His love is perfect, and it won't fail. Every promise will show up on our reel in some way, somehow, some day. It showed up on my reel when I was anticipating a situation that historically had left me feeling anxious and overwhelmed, because her love had failed me. I had noticed that in certain scenarios, dread would come to the surface of my mind without me even noticing or thinking about it, and without reason. This time was no different. That old familiar knot hit the bottom of my stomach as I anticipated an upcoming interaction. A lump in my throat got caught and I began to rehearse what might happen in the days ahead that could leave me repeating an old mantra: I won't be enough, my expectations for good will come up short leaving me hurt, disappointed, and somewhat anxious. In those moments of dreaded anticipation, my heart and mind collided with one short verse in one short chapter nearly smack in the middle of the Bible.

"God's unfailing love is great, and it is intended for us,
and His faithfulness to His promises knows no end. Praise the Eternal!"
Psalm 117:2 The Voice

Psalm 117 has only two verses. It's easily overlooked for obvious reasons. Until it's noticed, and then its truth can't be forgotten. God's love is unfailing. In the original language, the Hebrew word for that kind of love is "hesed." It's very difficult to translate into English for it has a wide range of meanings: mercy and kindness, goodness and favor, steadfast, everlasting, faithful.[56] Hesed is best described as God's merciful kindness. It's a love that cannot neglect or fail. And that kind of love is intended for us, designed and purposed for your heart and mine. His love cannot turn its back on us, and He will be faithful to His every promise today, tomorrow, and for all eternity. There's no return policy.

As I was turning the corner to walk into a new decade of living, Truth rushed to catch up and introduce me to Psalm 117, verse 2. I repeated the words like a mantra: *the unfailing love of God is intended for me, the unfailing love of God is intended for me, the unfailing love ....* and my mind meditated on each word. Unfailing is reliable, steady and sure. Intended carries the implication of planned. Hesed was for me, up close

Love
makes us
brave.

and personal. I received the hesed of God through my self-talk in place of rehearsing that critical voice and one's failure to love me.

As I declared the unfailing love of God over myself and the upcoming situation, my mind was renewed! Her words had empowered insecurity in my soul. His words began to empower confidence in the same internal space. The wrong pattern of thinking that often hit repeat in my mind; I won't do this right, I can't do this well, I must be perfect to have value, began to dislodge itself. His words acted as WD40. The default thoughts and words that typically plague me in similar situations released themselves. I grew confident and more brave. It happened as I listened to *His* words coming from *my* mouth.

His promises are bread from heaven for the hunger fear creates. His love is different than her love - or his love - and its unfailing nature is intended for me, and for you!

So, what about you? Any chance your response to one whose love failed you has created a mantra that plays in your head when this or that happens? Sit with that. Whose love failed you and, more importantly, how has that impacted your expectation for what's happening now? Do you hear the voice of the one who failed you echo in your head with repetition? Pause a minute and process your answer to those questions.

Take a lesson from my diary and meditate on the truth about the One whose love cannot and will not let you down. Play it on repeat: *God's unfailing love is intended for me.* It promises to change you from the inside out. The unfailing love of the Lord is intended for us! It's for me! And for you! Every single day. All day long.

God will never ever respond to you like _____ (so-and-so). Fill-in-the-blank and know that God's love will never treat you like theirs did ... or didn't. Never! His love cannot, will not, fail you. It. Is. Intended. For. You.

Breathe and let that truth sink in.

> **Love makes us brave.**

Love makes us brave. Receiving love and encountering its benefits makes you and me braver versions of ourselves. Just ask Hagar, Sarah's maidservant (Genesis 16:6-16).

Come Out of Hiding

Before we talk about Hagar, let's talk about a key player in her story, Abraham. Actually, Abram was his name before God changed it. At the time of Hagar's story, God had not yet changed either Abram nor his wife, Sarai's name but, for ease of reading, I'll use their commonly known names: Abraham and Sarah.

Abraham was 75 years old when God promised him land and a son. He was 99 when God reminded Him of that promise, and 100 years old when he and Sarah welcomed their promised son, Isaac, into the world. There was a heap of trouble and heartache for Abraham in between the promise of a son and the actual birth of Isaac. Abraham and Sarah visited the Valley of Trouble again and again during those long 25 years of waiting, and then waiting some more with little-to-no hope in sight.

It's no wonder during their season of waiting, Sarah got it in her head that it was time for her and Abe to help God out if His promise of her bearing a child was going to be fulfilled. So, with no promise-turned-reality on the horizon and a barrenness every day since they said I do, the story takes a turn. As difficult as it is for us to wrap our heads around it, Sarah offers her maidservant, Hagar, to Abraham in hopes the family name, and God's promise, will be honored and fulfilled. Strange to us but very common in the culture in which they lived. A maidservant often carried a child for the family's sake. So, Hagar becomes pregnant with Abraham's first child. All seemed well, until it wasn't. There were serious ramifications for Hagar following Sarah's decision to help with the plans of God. The disappointment for Sarah was real, the need for Sarah to fix "the problem" was imaginary.

> **Disappointment is real, the need to fix the problem is imaginary.**

Once Hagar conceived, she began to treat her mistress Sarah with disdain. Being barren was shameful. A woman was made to feel like a failure. Hagar took the golden opportunity to press both realities in Sarah's face and heart causing Sarah to regret her intervention into the situation. She complained to Abraham about Hagar and strife consumed their hearts and home. Pregnant Hagar couldn't tolerate Sarah's cruelty, and in a moment of severe frustration, she ran away into the desert wilderness. I mean, where else? Where on earth is a servant in her culture to run? But like Hagar, we can never run where God can't find us. In fact, an angel of the Lord whom scholars agree was the spirit of Jesus Himself, found Hagar there and told her to return home, reassuring her that she would become the mother of a great nation.

There in the desert Hagar recognizes God as Jehovah El Roi which means, "God sees me" because He did. God found Hagar and saw her hurting heart and promised that, through the birth of her child, a great nation would become reality. He then instructed her to name her baby boy, Ishmael, which means "God hears me." His birth was heaven's declaration that the living God, the God of Abraham, sees and hears us. (Genesis 16:13). The God who sees and the God who hears is a personal God. Very personal.

Hagar's story is my story. Hagar's story is your story. Whether male or female, pregnant or never have been, fugitive or home body, Hagar's story is our story. Life will deal severely with every single one of us at some point, humbling and afflicting us, and we will literally or metaphorically flee from it all. Separating ourselves on occasion. Temporarily, that's okay. We are human. But seeing and hearing the God who sees and hears us will most often send us home to face our reality and wait on God's coming good.

The weight you and I bear can be heavy, sometimes chronic, and always heart-wrenching, just like it was for those in Abraham's household. When we run away, that's the time we look for God. Listen for His voice and be reminded that He sees you and sees me.

He never grows tired of asking us again and again: Where did you come from and where are you going? And when we answer that we're running away because we just can't take it anymore, He is kind and not judgmental. He stays and doesn't leave. But He also never grows tired of telling you and me to go back to humbly submit to Him in the hard relationship, the challenging situation, the chronic suffering. The Holy Spirit is ever wanting us to submit to what will make us more like the Son (Romans 8:29). Let me be clear, however, I am not advocating that you stay in a marriage or any other relationship to endure abuse of any kind. If you are in such a situation, seek help from a professional source.

He hears you and me, and not just our words of discouragement, but our heart of confusion and fear. He never ever tires of finding us right where we are and reminding us of who He is, and whose we are.

It's because of that, you and I can return and submit to the assignment of heaven. We can settle in our hearts that He is a God who sees and declares over us that even on our darkest and most difficult days - or in our moment of escaping reality – He sees us and therefore, we live (Job 19:25-27)!

In time, we will bear that which He planted in us for His glory – an Ishmael, convinced that God hears us as well. In fact, He declares over you and me today: I am Jehovah El Roi, the God who sees and I am a master at giving birth to Ishmaels, proof that I am also the God who hears.

There was a second time Hagar and Ishmael were both put out of Abe and Sarah's house. However, Hagar wasn't running away that time, she was asked to leave. Strife broke out between the two half-brothers much like it had between their mothers. Ishmael was making fun of Isaac (Genesis 21:9-11). Sarah was hot! She was mad and hurt and insisted that Abraham tell Hagar and Ishmael to leave the house. Although Abraham did, it grieved him to do so, it was heartbreaking, difficult for him. But God wasn't done talking to Abe. He breaks the silent heartache and in essence says: Abraham, don't let this situation grieve you nor make you fearful about the plight of your boy and his mother. Go ahead and do what Sarah is asking knowing that through Isaac you will still be the father of many nations *and* I will make a nation through Ishmael because he also is your offspring (Genesis 21:9-13).

Abraham's story is our story and God says the same about the situations grieving you and me right now. So lean in, this matters: the reason for which you're hurting may be valid, but you can tune your ear to hear the Voice of heaven speaking over you saying: _____ (insert your name) - do not let this grieve you, do not yield to fear because I have a promise that I'm going to keep! You wait. You watch. You'll see. My goodness will show up in the trouble that is breaking your heart! I have a promise with your name on it, and it will one day be your reality.

Here's the thing, fellow Jesus followers; we know that our God is a God who never ever goes back on His word, and always delivers on His promise! So, we can lift up our eyes and see Him who sees us! That's Hagar's story in a nutshell. She's the one who called God *Jehovah El Roi* for the first time, the God who sees *and* the God we see. He's the God who has His eyes on you and me. And the God whom we can see and know, all at the same time, wrapped up together in one Name. Hagar's story is your story. It's my story. And it gives us hope and makes us brave. Therefore, you can do what you think you can't. So, when you close this book, submit to the hardship. It will be worth your courageous determination to do so.

Never Alone

Jesus was clear that as long as we have breath, we will have trouble on earth. The Father was kind and gracious to send Him into our world as Emmanuel to suffer like we do, but worse. And to acknowledge our hardship, but better. Whatever we're facing, Jesus knows, and He is with us.

He alone is respite for your soul, and time with Him will be your best chance to catch your breath and keep going. He will never leave your side nor give up on you or those you love.

You, my friend, will never be left to run your race solo nor navigate trouble on your own. Because of Jesus, you and I are never ever alone.

Emmanuel is His name, and He came so that God could be with you and with me every step of the way in this race called life (Matthew 1:23).

The Man with the String of Encouraging Words

One lazy Saturday morning I just so happened to see a modern-day Emmanuel running with a young boy through the park by our house. As I turned the corner near the park in Greentree neighborhood while walking the dog, I noticed a group of families who were jogging, likely in a race of some kind as they were adorned in matching T-shirts. I felt Holy Spirit encouraging me to stop, take in the scene, and not just note it but ponder and ingest it. So, I did.

I noticed a young boy lagging way behind the others and a man, most likely his dad although I couldn't be certain, jogging very slowly in front of him. The boy was walking with his small frame bent over slightly and his left hand pressed into his side while the man's head kept turning back keeping his eye on the lad. His words were prodding the boy to catch up. He spoke simple words but difference-making all the same. Things like: "Come on, buddy, you can do this, I'll stay with you! I know it's hard. I know you're tired, but we can do this! We're almost there. I'll run with you. Run up here next to me, I'll slow down. Let's run together and see if we can catch up with the others." The man never let his string of encouraging words come to a stop.

Shortly, the little fella straightened his body and began to jog at a leisurely pace, aka snail's pace. Immediately I could hear the man declaring: "Good job, buddy! I knew you could do it! You've got this, we'll do it together. I think we can still catch the others. Come on, let's run ..." and on and on he went.

I'm not sure I caught every word accurately, but I heard enough for the Spirit to paint a beautiful picture in my soul of who Jesus wants to be in our lives especially when we fall behind and run alone.

We know that the Father instructed His only Son to leave heaven for a while in order to live on earth. His Son came for several reasons, including His intention to be among us so He could run with us, alongside us, to encourage us and make the difficulty of our lives less so; to be sure we never run alone. It's an incredible thing really. Life with Jesus is an incredible thing. A game-changer for this journey we call life.

Personally, I think God's getting a bad rap right now (not by all but by many) in being blamed for the bad happening all around us. The darkness we see in our world isn't from Him. There's an evil one, and there's God. The evil one loves all things death-inducing and God loves all things life-giving (John 10:10).

Even in death, Jesus brings life. Even in darkness, He brings light. Even in heartache, He brings hope. Even when damaged, He brings healing. And He runs alongside us in our race. He becomes our strength in weakness when what seems insurmountable is tempting us to give up and quit. Emmanuel runs with us and makes the race bearable: God with you and God with me.

What a picture turned reality. Emmanuel never once takes His eyes off of us and never lets His string of encouraging words take pause while we lag behind. He runs with you and me. And when we recognize His Presence, and hear His voice, while running the race we've been assigned, we can catch our breath, and keep going all the way to the finish line.

BREATHE DEEPLY

"And the Lord God formed man of the dust of the ground, and breathed into his nostrils the breath of life; and man became a living being."
Genesis 2:7

INHALE

Joshua 1:6-9

Psalm 56 (read it in The Passion Translation if possible)

Psalm 84

Isaiah 41:10-13

I Corinthians 16:13

1 Peter 5:6-11

EXHALE

- Choose a verse, a sentence or just a phrase from one of the passages above.[57]
- Write it down on something you can post in your home, office or car, or at least carry with you.
- Meditate on its meaning; think about it again and again (and again!) over the course of your day/week.
- Read it in context.
- Read it in other Bible versions; the Amplified and Passion Translation are favorites.
- Look up the meaning of the words that you want to better understand.
- Memorize the verse or passage.
- Let the verse or phrase run around on the inside of you until it becomes your very own, part of your DNA.
- Consider personalizing it by inserting your name, or praying it for yourself, someone else, or for a situation.

BENEDICTION

"Let the sunrise of your love end our dark night.

Break through our clouded dawn again!

*Only you can satisfy our hearts, filling us with
songs of joy to the end of our days.*

*We've been overwhelmed with grief; come now
and overwhelm us with gladness.*

Replace our years of trouble with decades of delight.

*Let us see your miracles again, and let the rising generation
see the glorious wonders you're famous for.*

O Lord our God, let your sweet beauty rest upon us.

*Come work with us, and then our works will endure;
you will give us success in all we do."*

Psalm 90:14-17 TPT

Pause. Be still. Breathe, and as you close this book, believe that Jesus is speaking over you saying,

"You've been taking care of yourself for so, so long. You've often felt alone and weary which is different than tired and weary. Feeling alone carries with it...

- an emotional weight that feels heavy
- an emptiness that feels anxious
- burdens for tomorrow that feel frightening
- a false sense of responsibility that feels real

"I am your Sabbath-Rest; the place you can stop, lay it all down, lean on Me, and breathe while you wait, and more change arrives. I invite you to rest. I will solve the problems with you. I will shush you and love you while you sit still. I will sing over you with joy as you receive my tender loving care. Change chokes.

"Waiting with no vision for tomorrow suffocates. I am your safe place in the waiting, and feeling safe always lets you breathe, and then breathe some more. Stay with Me awhile so you can catch your breath before getting back up to face what's next.

"I am your Sabbath rest. Come to Me, I wait with you. Bring your soul that's ever so weary from feeling alone and believing it's all up to you. Yoke with me. Learn from me. Breathe and breathe again even while you wait. I am safe. You are home, child, for I am your Sabbath-Rest."

ABOUT THE AUTHOR

Sherilyn Jameson is a voice of hope as an author and teacher, passionate about seeing lives transformed by God's Word and His Spirit. She and her husband, Dave, live in Oceanside, California, and are parents to two adult sons. Sherilyn is retired and enjoys reading, living by the beach, and being a nana.

NOTES

Front Matter

1   Oxford English Dictionary (2024). Respite. In *Oxford English Dictionary*. Retrieved from [OED website URL]. Accessed 06/12/2024

Introduction

2   Christianity.com, "Samaria: The Place Jesus Must Visit in John 4:4"

3   Cambridge Dictionary (2024). Respite. In Cambridge *Online Dictionary* Retrieved from [https://dictionary.cambridge.org/dictionary/english/respite#google_vignette]. Accessed 06/12/2024

Chapter 1

4   Strong, James. *The New Strong's Exhaustive Concordance of the Bible,* edited by Kohlenberger III, John R., Thomas Nelson, [H622]

5   *Strong's Concordance [G2293]*

6   Oxford Languages Online. Retrieved May 19, 2024, https://search.yahoo.com/searchfr=mcafee&type=E210US105G0&p=defnition+of+corage

7   *Strong's Concordance* [G5219]

8   Stephanie Esser, creator of the acronym B.O.P. (Breathe On Purpose), balancingelephants.com

9   The Bible Gateway app is a great resource.

Chapter 2

10 TerKeurst, L (2018). *It's Not Supposed to Be This Way: Finding Unexpected Strength When Disappointment Leaves You Shattered.* Thomas Nelson, Nashville, TN.

11 Gethsemane, Britannica.com

12 Tripp, P.D. (2017). Come Let Us Adore Him: A Daily Advent Devotional Crossway, Wheaton, IL, p. 22

13 TerKeurst, L (2018). *It's Not Supposed to Be This Way: Finding Unexpected Strength When Disappointment Leaves You Shattered.* Thomas Nelson, Nashville, TN, p. 34

14 The Bible Gateway app is a great resource for reading other versions of the Bible.

Chapter 3

15 www.enduring word.com "Job 1 – Job Endures His Loss"

16 Lewis, C.S. (2001) *A Grief Observed.* Harper One, New York, NY, p. 33

17 Strong's Concordance [H3068]

18 Strong's Concordance [H7138]

19 Strong's Concordance [H7665]

20 Strong's Concordance [H1793]

21 Bragg, P.C. & Bragg, P. (2004), *The Miracle of Fasting: Proven Through History* (50th ed). Bragg, p. 119

22 The Bible Gateway app is a great resource for reading other versions of the Bible.

Chapter 4

23 Strong's Concordance [H7673]

24 Strong's Concordance [H7673]

25 Greig, P. (2019). *How to Pray; A Simple Guide for Normal People.* NavPress, Colorado Springs, CO, p. 41

26 The Bible Gateway app is a great resource for reading other versions of the Bible.

27 Greig, P. (2019). *How to Pray: A Simple Guide for Normal People.* NavPress, Colorado Springs, CO, p. 20

Chapter 5

28 Curt Thompson explains Confessional Communities in detail in his book, *The Soul of Desire*

29 Thompson, C. (2021). The Soul of Desire: Discovering the Neuroscience of Longing, Beauty and Community. InterVarsity Press, London, England, p. 6

30 Note: Early on in Dave's journey with Parkinson's Disease (PD is the common abbreviation), I decided that when I feel really frustrated with Parkinson's, I would refer to Dave as Pete; Parkinson's Pete. All of my husband's names and nicknames are used in my writing; David, Dave, DJ

31 Brown, B. (2012) Daring Greatly: How the Courage to Be Vulnerable Transforms the Way We Live, Love, Parent, and Lead. Gotham Books, New York City, NY, p. 34

32 Internet/social media

33 Strong's Concordance [G2170]

34 Strong's Concordance [G2170]

35 The Bible Gateway app is a great resource for reading other versions of the Bible.

Chapter 6

36 Strong's Concordance [G3528]

37 The Bible Gateway app is a great resource for reading other versions of the Bible.

Chapter 7

38 Background information on Numbers 27 taken from a post, "Good Morning Girls" by blogger, Courtney Joseph

39 Blog.sony.edu; "Texting While Walking Can Be More Dangerous Than Distracted Driving." 06/12/2024

40 The Bible Gateway app is a great resource for reading other versions of the Bible.

Chapter 8

41 Spurgeon, Charles. "The Pillow and the Sword." In *The New Park Street Pulpit. Vol. 6, sermon 322. London: Passmore & Alabaster, 1860*

42 Johnston, C. (2020) Releasing Prophetic Solutions: Destiny Image, Shippensburg, PA, p. 75

43 The Passion Translation (2017) Psalm 16

44 Chambers, O. (1935). *My Utmost for His Highest.* Dodd, Mead & Company, Toronto, Canada

45 Sayers, Dorothy. The Greater Trumps. London: Victor Gollancz Ltd, 1932

46 Strong's G5236

47 The Bible Gateway app is a great resource for reading other versions of the Bible.

Chapter 9

48 Strongs (H5911)

49 Merriam-Webster. *Merriam-Webster Online Dictionary.*

50 Strong's Concordance [G2872]

51 christianity.com, *What is Yoke in The Bible? Meaning of Jesus Teaching,* April 23, 2024

52 Ortlund, D. (2020). *Gentle and Lowly: The Heart of Christ for Sinners and Sufferers.* Crossway, Wheaton IL, pp. 19-21

53 Shared in a sermon by one of the Evangelical Sisters of Mary at Canaan in the Desert, Phoenix, AZ, 1991

54 The Bible Gateway app is a great resource for reading other versions of the Bible.

Chapter 10

55 Savard, L (1992). *Shattering Your Strongholds: Freedom From Your Struggles.* Bridge-Logos, North Brunswick, NJ, p. 51

56 Strong's Concordance [H2617]

57 The Bible Gateway app is a great resource for reading other versions of the Bible.

www.ingramcontent.com/pod-product-compliance
Lightning Source LLC
Chambersburg PA
CBHW070656130626
46553CB00005B/1731